"*Made to Lead* is exquisitely writt[en] and passion. Any woman strugglin[g] any man who rejects the Divine call of woman to be spokespersons for the Lord, needs to read this book."
— *Joan S. Parrott, Executive Minister, First Baptist Church of Hampton, Virginia*

"Nicole Martin is a voice, a gift, a young sage, a positive force for the transforming of the church for creative ministry in the 21st century. This is a must-read for women and men who care to see the church relevant again."
— *Frank A. Thomas, Professor of Preaching, Christian Theological Seminary, Indianapolis*

"Biblical examples, personal stories, practical tips, and devotional prayers inspire us to imagine new leadership possibilities and makes *Made to Lead* a practical must-read for those who want the Body of Christ to be blessed by the leadership gifts of all its parts."
— *Eustacia Moffett Marshall, Pastor, Faith Point Fellowship, Greensboro, NC*

"Nicole Martin reminds us that the gifts God gives are not gender specific. ... Reading this book will not only help women in ministry to be unleashed but will unleash men to be partners in ministry and not competitors."
— *Rodney L. Cooper, Kenneth and Jean Professor of Discipleship and Leadership, Gordon-Conwell Theological Seminary, Charlotte*

"This is the book I wish I'd had back when I was first called to ministry!"
— *Jolin Wilks McElroy, Senior Pastor, First Christian Church, Charlotte, and Founder, Dilworth Soup Kitchen*

For my precious daughters, Addison and Josephine

MADE
– TO LEAD –

EMPOWERING WOMEN FOR MINISTRY

To Jack and Lisa —
You were made for this!
May God continue to bless you
as He moves through you
to bless others.

NICOLE MASSIE MARTIN

Your Sister in Christ —

CBP®

ST. LOUIS, MISSOURI

Cover art and design: Bidemi (Bd) Oladele

CBPBooks.com

Print: 9780827223677
EPUB: 9780827223684   EPDF: 9780827223691

Printed in the United States of America

Contents

Section 3: Lead with Purpose!

Foreword

Many works attempt to articulate concern for the obstacles confronting persons in ministry, but fewer combine survey data, anecdotal stories, and analysis of biblical texts. It is exactly this combination that Nicole Massie Martin has been able to effect. Steeped as she is in sound biblical theology, the author has given us a careful study that may, itself, be valued for a time to come for use with varied audiences. Not only is this a useful tool assisting women who are preparing for public ministry but it potentially serves to advise men, congregants, and pulpit search committees of the many barriers to be overcome. Although the present work routinely references both well-known and lesser-known texts of women in scripture, it is not solely about them. Instead it represents a genuinely original work.

What strikes us at once is the comprehensive character of the current undertaking. Some contemporary books deal solely with the inner life of the minister, but this one deals with an astonishing variety of external and internal factors. Much of its freshness of treatment arises from the ready identification any woman in ministry is likely to have with the anecdotal examples. The author has presented a wide spectrum of experience from sacred space to practical techniques for organizing one's ministry experiences. Since the finished product is the outcome of careful thinking, it is not the sort of book that can be shelved and dashed off quickly. It lends itself to use as a manual for students in pastoral care as well as the object of small group discussions.

Scripture and anecdotal examples are not the only fountain from which the author draws. A careful reader will recognize a large indebtedness to the author's own willingness to be transparent. As with all good works, reading this book stirs one to want to read more on the subject or to somehow take action toward creating healthier options for women and all persons in ministry.

The greatest problems of our times are not technological, because we are continuously addressing these through innovation. Matters of polity and economics may not be our most overwhelming challenges. The greatest problems are moral and spiritual and what we as humans do to other humans even when we are well-meaning. It is for this reason that I welcome a really well-thought-out discourse on the cultivation of the life and spirit of the woman preparing for service in public ministry.

Bishop Cynthia Rembert James, Ph.D., D.Min.

Introduction

Why Tackle the Topic of Women's Leadership Now?

Look at what is already taking place in churches around the world: Women are leading. Women are preaching. Women are serving God in ministry. Women whom God has called are changing people's lives daily: through a woman's sermon, people are accepting Christ. Through the ministry of a woman, families and couples are being reconciled. By the works of women in ministry, God is shaping the landscape of the kingdom of God. This trend of women in church leadership positions is becoming stronger and more prevalent.

All over the world, women declare the words of the prophet Isaiah, "The spirit of the Lord God is upon me, because the Lord has anointed me."[1] Every day, some woman somewhere recognizes that God has called and anointed her to serve in ministry. This calling of God upon the life of any individual is not optional. It is an undeniable, unavoidable calling that must be answered. Some women who are called by God don't even believe that they should preach, but they cannot deny God's calling. Some women struggle with their qualifications, but them, too, the Lord has anointed. When women answer God's call, they often face opposition regarding the validity of their calling. Having been inundated with women-demeaning theories, opinions, life experiences, and isolated scriptures, they often spend years debating the authenticity of God's Spirit upon them and the authority or reach of that anointing. This book is not about whether or not women can be called. This book is about how women can prepare themselves for ministry once they accept that calling. If you're one of those women, I've written this book for you.

Background

I am the proud product of a family of boundary-breakers, matriarchs, and nurturing men of God. I know that I am where I am as a result of my mother, Dr. Elfreda Massie, who is an entrepreneur and scholar, and my father, Rev. Leonard Massie Jr., a pastor, educator, and administrator. Together they instilled within me values of education, determination, and passion in a life with Christ. Although I spent most of my childhood in church or playing church, I never thought that I would be the child that followed in my father's footsteps. I am the older of two girls and my sister was the one that everyone said would eventually become a preacher. Yet throughout my childhood and adolescence, I could not fight the fact that I felt God's pull toward the things of the church. I loved worship. I enjoyed teaching the Word and discipling others. I desired an authentic relationship with Christ and I even had "Jesus is Real" printed on my high school band jacket. Yes, I was the "Jesus Lover," and no matter how hard I tried to fit in, I always stood apart.

At a young age, I also had a gift to lead, and positions of leadership usually found me wherever I went. Throughout my years in school, I led everything from gospel choirs to Bible studies, but I never imagined that I would be called to church leadership. After all, I was a girl, and in my Baptist church, the women were typically relegated to music, and women's or children's ministries. Although raised to believe that I could do and be anything I wanted, I wasn't sure that God would call me to lead in the church. While my parents' encouragement pushed me to follow my passions and dreams, I had friends who openly frowned upon women who wanted to pastor. Sure, women could run for president of God's United States, but no women should think that she could lead in God's church.

So when I first accepted God's calling to pastoral leadership and vocational ministry, I wrestled with what it meant to be a woman in ministry with a calling to serve the whole church, both men and women. I struggled with the opinions of friends and other women in church who would say: "I believe that you are called, but women should only teach women." "If God put men as heads of the household, why would He choose a woman to be the head of the church?" My parents taught me that I could break through any and every boundary and that there were no conditions on my calling. Although I didn't believe what other people said, the constant questions and doubts often weighed on my heart.

I had not seen very many women preachers or pastors, and I wondered whether God could really use me in this vocation. Did God make a mistake in calling me? Was I only supposed to impact the lives of women and not men? As a young single woman, my primary concern at that time was making sure that I was obedient in serving God in the authority I had been given. I spent many years researching various views on women in ministry, not only for my own benefit but also as a means of building an arsenal of responses for those who questioned my calling. While my male counterparts were discovering how they could prepare for vocational ministry, not having questioned for a moment whether such a calling was legitimate, I was busy trying to assess whether the complementarian or egalitarian view of women in ministry best suited what I believed God was calling me to do.[2]

When I entered seminary, I could not help but notice the stark difference between young men and women engaged in the work of ministry preparation. In general, young women came to the seminary environment still justifying their places as ministers of the gospel. Like me, they spent much of their time inwardly building up the courage to move forward, while young men generally spent more time outwardly developing connections that were in line with where and how they felt called to serve.

The time spent in inward affirmation often led women to feel more confident in their relationships with Christ, but not having spent time building the necessary external connections, they were often without the network necessary to find employment within the church or advocates for their development. I watched as gifted women went back into banking or decided to return to secular fields after graduating from seminary since there were no ministry opportunities available for them. I saw gifted men get drafted to pastor churches while still in seminary.

This duality of experience made me realize that the way that men and women approached their calling determined how they processed the seminary experience. For many men, seminary was the last step before entering full-time pastoral ministry. It was a rite of passage; it was a chance to build their portfolio for preaching and teaching in order to launch them into the ministry position of their dreams. For many women, seminary was a place of discernment and discovery. It was a time for God to prove to them that they were qualified and to test out the possibilities of where they could serve. As a result, it was not uncommon to see young seminary men applying for churches and preparing for ordination exams in their first and second years of school while women often waited until closer to graduation, if they took that step at all.

It wasn't until my first years in ministry that I recognized the impact of this discernment and preparation process on the careers of women in ministry. Women, burdened with the task of validating their calling, often missed out on being developed for that call. As a result, I saw many women graduating from seminary and returning to secular jobs, serving as ministry volunteers, or taking "nonmanagerial" positions at a church when they desired so much more. Among those women who do go on to ministry positions after seminary, often even high-capacity women leaders spend years in low-capacity positions with few leadership development opportunities. On the other hand, high-capacity male leaders are often granted leadership opportunities and training by mentors, both inside and outside of the church, even before their careers begin. They often enter seminary with a pastor or group of pastors that mentor them through to the placement process, while young women often pursue their educations without the support of family or their church leaders. While young men are being developed to serve as pastors and ministry leaders, young women, and especially those in more independent denominations, are often unmentored and not helped by a community of supporters in discerning where their gifts will be best used. As a result, women must fight hard for pastoral and managerial positions that come with authority, power, and seniority. Even today, women are still underrepresented in pastoral ministry and managerial ministry staff positions in almost every Christian denomination.

This is what you're up against. And yet the good news is: you were made for this.

The Stained Glass Ceiling

Such underrepresentation of women in positions of authority, leadership, power, and influence is of course hardly restricted to the church. In early 2013, Sheryl Sandberg, the chief operating officer of Facebook, forced into the open the truth that women are underrepresented in leadership in nearly every vocational field. Citing differences such as gaps in ambition, gender-related leadership styles, and the disparate burdens of parenthood, Sandberg's goal was to help women overcome the obstacles and embrace the challenges of upward mobility. From her perspective, men are able to excel in leadership primarily because they are not afraid to take risks. They look for opportunities and believe that they are capable of succeeding in higher-level jobs, even those beyond their actual abilities. In recalling a business weekend event, she stated, "The men were focusing on how to manage a business and the women were focusing on how to manage a career. The men wanted answers and the women wanted permission to help."[3] Sandberg emphasized that, despite growing efforts over the years to equalize the corporate playing fields, the leadership gap between men and women in power still exists in corporations today.

Women have beaten the odds in so many areas and made progress in recent decades, as is evidenced by the increased earning potential of women and the media's depiction of men in more nurturing roles, for example. Some could argue that, unlike previous generations, we raise our young women today with a more intentional understanding that nothing is impossible for them. Whereas our grandmothers were raised to believe that marriage would be their ticket to a secure life, today we tell our girls that they can create their own destinies and build their careers, with or without husbands. We tell our girls that they can take on any career and encourage them to excel in subjects far beyond the typical gender-specific fields.

Even role models for young girls look different now than they have in years past. Today's young women can look almost anywhere to see women working and taking leadership positions in government, education, corporations, healthcare, sports management, and more. Thanks to women from previous generations who paved the way, our young women should be able to see themselves achieving their goals with great success. At the same time, Sandberg indicates that young women in their late teens and twenties[4] still struggle with seeing themselves as leaders or in leadership positions within their chosen career fields:

> Millennial women are less likely than Millennial men to agree that the statement, "I aspire to a leadership role in whatever field I ultimately work" describes them very well. Millennial women were also less likely than their male peers to characterize themselves as "leaders," "visionaries," "self-confident," and "willing to take risks."[5]

Giving girls confidence, helping them to dream is one thing. Seeing their mothers and peers attain those top leadership positions is another—and it still doesn't happen for women the way it does for men. Women still have to fight for their spot. And sometimes the women around them will consider them "uppity" and "bossy" for doing so. Having aspirations is still not a safe space or attitude for girls.

In an ideal world, this safe space would be the church. However, in many cases, even the church is riddled with negative systems of sexism and oppressions regarding the development of women in leadership. The church, the Body of Christ, is designed to operate with all people working in all spiritual gifts. God has given to men and women the gifts and talents necessary to further the kingdom, as the Bible instructs[6]. Yet for many women, the place that should be a safe haven for developing their gifts of leadership is the place that stifles their potential.

The metaphor of the "stained glass ceiling" describes this reality. As the proverbial "glass ceiling" exists in corporate America, the "stained glass ceiling" exists in the church, limiting women from climbing to positions of high authority and power. Author and self-defined feminist theologian Gina Messina-Dysert set out to discover the truth about opportunities for women in the Catholic Church. Although her findings gave a small glimmer of hope for women seeking greater leadership and service, it also confirmed the challenges that exist and may remain for Catholic women who sense God's calling for church governance and leadership. Unfortunately, this metaphor of the "stained glass ceiling" is very much the reality in the Protestant church as well. According to a survey on The State of Women in Baptist Life 2010, the number of women graduating from seminary and being ordained has increased and continues to increase over the years,[7] but at the same time, the Associated Baptist Press reports that theologically trained and ordained women in ministry are more likely to be employed in staff positions holding less power and authority than their male counterparts (i.e., children and youth ministry, education, women's ministry, and so on).[8] So if more women are entering ministry and being ordained, what is holding them back from the kind of leadership success men have? Are they underprepared? Is the church still biased against women leaders?

A 2014 article posted by The United Methodist Church gives some clues. It reported survey findings that indicated an overall increase in the number of women ordained and placed in pastoral leadership.[9] The most dramatic improvement was seen among women of color who are now receiving local church appointments at higher rates than ever before. Yet the survey also revealed that the primary reason why women are leaving pastoral ministry is to pursue ministries beyond the church, and that "the number of women clergy citing 'lack of support from the hierarchical system' as their reason for leaving actually increased," especially among African-American, Asian and Asian-American women.[10] These statistics indicate that while the number of women accepting the call to ministry is growing, the systems in place to support and develop their callings are not.

This fact becomes even more important as it relates to African-American women considering or entering ministry. Such women have built upon the foundation laid by Julia Foote, who on May 20, 1894, became the first African-American woman to be ordained as a deacon by the African Methodist Episcopal Zion church. In nearly every African-American church, women make up the overwhelming majority of the membership. They fill almost every role in ministry as teachers, evangelists, counselors, deacons, "deaconesses," missionaries, cooks, intercessors, and administrators.[11] As they have been throughout history, African-American women are pivotal in the development and sustainability of the church. While it is difficult to get accurate statistics on the number of minority women entering seminary, a study from 1992 revealed that African-American women made up as much as 35 percent of all women enrolling in seminary.[12] Research by Courtney Lyons published in 2013 showed that women made up nearly half of all African-American seminarians in 2012.[13] Based on this data, it is clear that women may soon be the majority of African-American seminarians.

However, this same research shows that women make up only about 1 percent of African-American Baptist pastors; their numbers in other denominations remain low as well. As the number of women in seminary increases, the opportunities to be developed and placed as pastoral leaders have not. Many of the churches where they seek to serve either have no formal development and placement plan for women in ministry or refuse to affirm women's callings altogether. Since the African-American female demographic tends to represent the smallest constituency in mainline denominations that provide clear processes for training and placement (Presbyterian, Lutheran, Episcopal, Methodist, and so on), such women often receive the least support for ministerial development and mentorship in the calling of church leadership.

There has not been much research done on the numbers of Latina, Native American, Asian, or Asian-American women entering ministry,[14] but one can speculate that their path to development is very similar to that of other women. Regardless of how progressive our culture becomes, the church still remains deeply rooted in traditional patriarchal household values.

For many opponents of women in ministry, the idea of having a woman as a pastor seems threatening. If the church is a place where adults and children can see positive examples of what family should look like, for those with patriarchal values it is very difficult to justify a woman at the helm. Despite the large numbers of contemporary examples where women lead in both the workplace and the home, many conservative churches still believe that the idea of a woman in leadership opposes what "church" is all about. For women seeking leadership within the church, it appears the obstacles of promotion and development in the world are not too different to the church.

Overview of This Book

We in the church are in need of real-life examples, guidance, and ideas of how to help develop women like you for successful church leadership. Young women need direction on how to sustain the strength of God's anointing in contexts that may not fully support their development. More seasoned women need practical information to help them move from where they are to where they want to be in ministry. Men and congregations who support women in ministerial leadership positions need resources to help them properly articulate and support God's work in the lives of female leaders. I have designed this book to help women leaders understand that we were made for the call of Christ to lead the church in the direction of God's calling for the next level of ministry.

The first part of this book focuses on preparing women to lead in the church. The first chapter in this section deals with what it means for God to call women to leadership. The second chapter looks at how God developed women in the Bible for positions of leadership, with special attention to the role of Jesus in leadership development. It develops a theological basis around women in leadership. The third chapter describes the current climate of church leadership for women, and emphasizes the real-life challenges that women in ministry face.

The second part of the book focuses on specific keys to successful leadership development for women in ministry. Using information gathered from surveys conducted for women entering ministry, each chapter elaborates on what women believe they need most in leadership development—confidence, love, sacred space, and mentorship—and how they can achieve it. Chapter 4 discusses the importance of cultivating confidence throughout one's ministry caree. Chapter 5 explores what it means for a woman in ministry to have a love life, specifically related to families, singleness, and self. Chapter 6 helps the reader understand what it means to create "sacred space" or circles of peers in which women can be free to share in the struggles and joys of Christian leadership. Chapter 7 deals with the role of mentorship and the significance of finding male and female mentors.

The third part of the book focuses on "where to go from here" as women leaders. Chapter 8 is all about finding a place to serve in ministry and the various options for women who are called and prepared. Chapter 9 discusses the importance of owning your body as a means of successful ministry leadership. Chapter 10 encourages women to cultivate other passions and desires outside of ministry to avoid burnout, stay healthy, explore their talents, and maintain a diverse and personally enlivening portfolio of interests.

Speaking to the crowd on the Day of Pentecost, Peter attempted to explain what God was doing. What the crowd saw with their eyes were people they believed were unqualified, but what they heard with their ears was God's Word spoken in their own languages. Immediately, some cast doubt on this miracle, claiming that those speaking must have been drunk. In response, Peter boldly reminded them of what God had already promised through the prophet Joel:

> In the last days, God says, I will pour out my Spirit on all people. Your sons and daughters will prophesy, your young men will see visions, your old men will dream dreams. Even on my servants, both men and women, I will pour out my Spirit in those days, and they will prophesy.[15]

It's as if Peter is trying to remind them that the urgency of the times called for drastic measures from God. The message of the gospel is too important to leave in just one language, but needs to be spoken so that all can understand. It's also too important to be articulated only by men. God will use both men and women, young and old to preach this life-giving Word to a dying world. There is too much at stake for us to drag our feet debating whether or not God is able to use whomever God chooses.

The time to prepare leaders like you for the future of the church is now. The process of developing called women like you to pastoral leadership has to happen now. Today, we must roll up our sleeves and advance the kingdom of God. Today, enlisted by the Holy Spirit, men and women like you must put aside doubt and strap on the garments of leadership to equip the church for what lies ahead. If there were ever a season for women to be boldly equipped for service, that season is right now.

You were made for this time. You were made for this task. So, let's roll up our sleeves and get to work!

SECTION 1

GET READY!

1

Made for the Call

If you're reading this book, it's because you are one of the brave women who has accepted the fact that God can use you (or one of the brave male supporters of such an amazing woman). You have agreed to serve the Lord in ways that you can't even fathom at this moment. You've said "yes" to a process that is unfamiliar, yet you're ready and willing to navigate this unfamiliar territory. You have agreed to a lifestyle that may seem hard to imagine. You've reached a major milestone in your life of which you should feel proud! You have accepted God's call.

Those who are called by God have said yes to . . . God knows what! Only God knows the details and purpose for which each one of us is called. We've agreed to a future that looks fuzzy to us but is crystal clear to God. With all of these ambiguities and doubts, it's amazing that you and so many women like you still have the strength and grace to say "yes!" Don't worry: you are not alone. You were made for this call!

To be called by God is to be set apart for the work of ministry in a unique way. It means that you have been appointed and anointed for a work in God's kingdom that will draw on your past experiences along with future training in leadership, teaching, preaching, and a host of other gifts, talents, and abilities. While everyday there are many people who accept God's calling, many others still wrestle with and deny the calling on their lives. Unfortunately, many of those happen to be women.

The reality for many of us women is that we know deep inside that God is calling us to lead ministries in the church, but we allow internal and external obstacles to keep us from embracing that call. Why? Some women have not seen many examples of women in ministry and cannot quite believe that this calling is for them. They may attribute masculine qualities to ministry and feel that they are not strong enough, tall enough, or don't have a voice loud enough to lead. Other women feel that who they are as mothers or young women prevents them from being fully used by God. They see people working at the church day and night and suppose that mothers couldn't possibly fill those shoes. They see married couples collaborating in leadership and assume that singles could never manage that kind of pressure or they see singles leading with a freedom they don't feel as a married person or parent.

Other women struggle with the pressures to measure up to televised, photoshopped images of women in society. No matter how old or young, whether single or married, we women constantly face insecurities, and we fear that we are not pretty enough, smart enough, thin enough, or tall enough to be accepted by others.

Once we do manage to wrap our heads around those external stressors, then we confront our internal struggles as well. We ask: Can God really use me, knowing where I have been and what I've been through? Considering all of my issues and weaknesses, does God really want me to lead? More fundamentally, does the Bible really endorse the notion of women in ministry? Sometimes we have our doubts. Even the most progressive women wrestle with what to make of scriptures that suggest women should remain quiet in the church or only minister to other women, not exercising authority over a man.[1] And then we wrestle with self-esteem and acceptance issues. In effect, saying "yes" to God also means saying "yes" to ourselves. It means accepting that who we are is good enough for God.

> In effect, saying "yes" to God also means saying "yes" to ourselves.

These concerns may be valid. But they leave out the most important thing: that God is the One who initiates the call. Do we believe that God knows what God is doing in calling us? Do you believe? If God is the One behind the small whisper in your heart, then surely God believes that you can do what you are called to do. This means that (especially with some training) the ideas that come into your mind as you read scripture are good enough to be put into a sermon; that the advice that you give and the listening skills you have can be formalized in a counseling session; that the programs that you've developed, the discernment you exercise in talking to people, and the prayers you've prayed for those in need are all valid gifts that God can use in ministry leadership. Yes, God can and will use you! Yes, you were made for this calling.

Consider Sharon's[2] story. Sharon was always leading someone, ever since she was a child. She can recall lining her dolls up one by one and teaching them with authority at just four years old. As she grew up, Sharon always felt drawn to the church. On some Sundays, she was the only one in her household who walked down to the local church where she sat in the back and enjoyed the worship experience. She developed relationships there and eventually became involved as a junior usher. By the time she went off to college, she had served in most of the ministries in the church and enjoyed talking about God to her family and friends, most of whom assumed that she was being brainwashed by the church.

Sharon went off to college knowing that she was different. As much as she tried to fit in, she was always recognized as the "church girl" and the go-to for prayer and an encouraging word.

When a professor suggested that she consider seminary or a vocation in ministry, she balked, believing that she could never be qualified to serve in such an important field. Growing up, she had only seen one woman in ministry and had never felt a connection to her. Instead, she decided to follow her accounting degree all the way to a reputable firm where she was able to do church ministry on the side and make a living for herself.

After ten years of working in the accounting field, Sharon could fight her call no longer. Both internally and externally, she knew that God was calling her to serve in ministry leadership. On the inside, she could no longer fight the fact that her heart and mind were connected to God and to the church, even when she was at work. On the outside, she was tired of wrestling with the people who assumed that she was a nun or a minister because they caught a glimpse of her true passion. So one Saturday afternoon during her devotional time, she finally said "yes" to God and to her call. She agreed to the fact that God wanted to use her to serve more fully and lead more intentionally in the context of God's kingdom. Beyond that, however, she had no idea what exactly she was called to do or how to start the process.

So, what exactly does it mean for you to be called by God? Ask yourself the following questions:

1. Do you sense an internal wrestling that pushes you to serve God in ways that go beyond where you are and what you are doing now?

2. Do you read scriptures thinking about how they apply to your life and the lives of others?

3. Do your friends, family, or faith community leaders affirm the work of God in your life as a minister or leader?

4. Would you serve in a capacity that requires you to share the gospel, teach the scriptures, offer spiritual guidance, and serve the people, even if you didn't get paid?

5. Do you often find yourself excelling in leadership positions at work, church, or school?

If you answered positively to the questions above, God may be calling you to serve in ministry leadership.

Biblical Observations

Fortunately for us, the Bible is full of examples of God calling the least likely and using them with great purpose and power. Whether you are tall or short, soft-spoken or loud, a homebody or party animal, there are scriptures that remind us that God can still find you and call you wherever you are.

Hagar[3]

Hagar was an Egyptian slave girl. She was sold to Sarai's family and was destined to fulfill someone else's dreams. She was overlooked, unappreciated, and underestimated. No one cared who she was. She was to be known by what she could do and her function was simple: to serve her mistress Sarai and do whatever she was asked. It was a challenging existence and just when she thought that her life would be forever abased, she was asked to do something unbelievable: she was asked to bear a child for her mistress.

Having no say in the matter, Hagar did as she was told and conceived a child with her master, Abram. She finally began to experience another side of life. Instead of being at the bottom, Hagar began to rise to the top. The one who was trained always to think less of herself finally began to think more. The Bible tells us that when she knew she was pregnant, she began to despise her mistress. This "puffed up" sense of self eventually led to punishment and abuse from the family she knew so well. Feeling trapped and threatened, Hagar did the only thing she could to protect herself and the child growing within her: she ran away.

She ran with no clear direction or purpose. All she knew was that she needed to get away. Once she got into the desert, reality probably hit her hard. She had no food, she had no resources, and she didn't know anyone who could help her to deliver her child. Feeling lost and alone, Hagar sat down at a spring, most likely preparing to die. But it was there at the spring on the side of the road that God met her. In the midst of her despair, God called her. God called her by name, gave her directions, and assured her with the promise that everything would be all right. In essence, God affirmed that Hagar, the servant of Sarai, was made for a future and an impact that would be greater than anything she could imagine. This divine encounter would make Hagar the first person in the Old Testament to give God a name: El Roi, meaning "the God who sees."

Life Application

Hagar may not stand out on the top ten list of leaders in the Bible, but she was one of the first women

> The call of God meets us in spite of where we've been, what we've done, and who we used to be.

who experienced what it meant to be called by God. As women accepting God's calling, we can identify with Hagar's wrestling with position, power, and even her obedience to do what may not have made sense at the time. Hagar embodies the feeling of isolation that can come with leadership, the feeling of despair that can come when we feel like our options are few, the desire to protect our children and those who have been entrusted to us, and even the sense of oppression that can come from being viewed by what we do and not by who we are. Her story is important to all women because through her, God reminds us that we are destined for so much more than we can see or imagine.

One of the first things Hagar's story teaches us is the fact that *God knows where we've been.* Sometimes, we struggle to accept God's calling because of the women we used to be. We can be paralyzed by the past and halted by our wounds, believing that these things disqualify us from serving God and God's people. We wonder whether God made an error and called us by accident, mistaking us for a better and more holy version of ourselves. But Hagar reminds us that God knows everything about us and still chooses to call us by name. The call of God meets us in spite of where we've been, what we've done, and who we used to be. As women redeemed by God, we are reminded of God's all-sufficient grace that equips us for everything that lies ahead.

Hagar's story also teaches us that *God knows where we're going.* The angel told Hagar to return to her mistress, Sarai, because God was preparing to bless her in unimaginable ways. He said, "I will increase your descendants so much that they will be too numerous to count" (Genesis 16:10 NIV). God not only knew where Hagar had been, but God also knew exactly where she needed to go. While it may not seemed logical or desirable to return, God did not send her back empty-handed. Instead, God sent Hagar back equipped with a promise and a vision for life that extended beyond anything she could imagine.

It is so good to know that God calls us from where we've been to places and spaces much bigger than ourselves. While the future may look uncertain and the details may not be completely clear, we carry the assurance of knowing that God knows the trajectory of the call. God knows the people we need to see, the places we need to go, and the tools we need to get there. The best part is that what God has in store for those who heed the call is always greater than what we can imagine.

God knows where we've been, God knows where we're going, and Hagar's story also reminds us that *God knows what we need.* This truth from Hagar's story is essential to every woman's call. Hagar needed something important from God; she needed to see and know the One who called her. God met her deepest needs, allowing her to find new purpose and meaning for her life and for her child. Having accepted the words of the angel, Hagar returned to raise her son in the knowledge of who God called him to be: the one who was called would nurture the call of another. By God's grace, your calling can be the spark that encourages someone else to accept their calling and live out their fullest potential in life.

Lastly, I believe that the story of Hagar also teaches us that in every calling, *God seeks to reveal more of God's self to us*. At the conclusion of this divine encounter, Hagar named God and declared, "I have now seen the One who sees me" (Genesis 16:13 NIV). Her calling positioned her to know God in a way that she had never known before.

You may not know it, but God has special treasures for those who bravely embrace the truth of God's calling. By saying "yes" to God, you are positioned to have a relationship with the Lord that exceeds what you have experienced in the past. Embracing God's call may not make you a millionaire or lead you to the center stage of life. However, scriptures remind us that those who are called to lead God's people are invited into a sacred relationship with God. They are given unique gifts and covered with an anointing that allows them to do whatever God calls them to do. From this, we understand that *God has so much in store for those who are called!*

As you consider your calling, take a few moments to respond to the following questions:

1. How do you know that God has called you?

2. What obstacles or questions come to your mind that you believe could disqualify you from embracing the call?

3. What principles from the story of Hagar resonate most with you?

4. What is God calling you to do in response to what you have read?

Summary

While every call is different, there are similarities that draw all of us together. No matter who you are or where you've been, our scriptures affirm that God can use you. If you are called or are wrestling with a call to serve in ministry leadership, you should know that you are not alone. God sends us community to affirm and clarify the specifics of the calling so that we will know the best fit for our gifts. You are surrounded by a cloud of witnesses, both men and women, who boldly declare that your calling is not just about you, it is also about what God wants to do *through* you. You have accepted the calling to perform a unique work in the kingdom of God. You are anointed to serve people who will respond to God's voice through you. My sister, God has opened a door of opportunity and for now all you have to do is say "yes!" You were made for this!

> *Lord, thank you for loving me enough to call me into greater service for You. Although I'm not certain of where the call will lead me, I am confident that as you were with Hagar, so you will be with me. Open my eyes to see you more clearly, my ears to hear your voice, and my arms to embrace all that you have in store for my life. Amen.*

2

Developing Leaders Like Jesus

While in college, I was asked to lead a Bible study on campus. I had no idea what I was doing, but for some reason, I couldn't let it go. Or I should say, it wouldn't let me go. After a period of wrestling, I decided to give it a try. For weeks, I would sit by myself waiting for people to show up. Not one person came; nope, not one. I even made cookies and lit candles! While people would stop by to grab a cookie, no one was convinced to stay. So, I decided to do what I had come to do: study the Bible. For weeks, I would sit there with my candles and cookies in the dorm lounge, the chairs in a circle and study the Word of the Lord... alone. In retrospect, I know that God was using those times to build a foundation of scripture in my heart.

One evening, after a riveting Bible study with just myself, I ran into one of the other residents in the dorm. She was a Christian; we went to the same church. When she asked how things had gone with my Bible study, I told her honestly that no one had come, but that I had enjoyed my time with God. I joked that maybe God was trying to tell me to change out my scented candles. She smiled and said, "Well, you know that God does not want women to be in leadership over a man, right?" I was speechless; that had never crossed my mind. She implied that the reason for my lack of success was because I was doing something that was unnatural and certainly unbiblical for women to do.

As a young college student on fire for God, it had never occurred to me that God did not want me to lead. I had never wondered whether or not God could use me in leadership and did not question God's ability to use me to minister to both men and women. Yet, after that conversation I began to doubt. This doubt sent me on a journey to discover that there was a whole world of debate about women in ministry, often led by negative views from women. So many perspectives, so many views, so many opinions and all of them using the very same biblical texts! How can you decide what God is saying when everyone uses the same verses to argue different points?

Fortunately, I believe that Jesus models for us the fact that He affirms, calls, and develops women for ministry leadership. The Jesus who called me to start a Bible study as preparation for ministry is the same Jesus who continues to prepare women for ministry today. Through the ministry of Jesus, women leaders can be confident that they are exactly where they need to be.

Biblical Observations

The climate for women during biblical times was challenging, to say the least. At best, women were considered leaders in specific contexts because of their fathers or husbands or their work in the home. At worst, women were property; they were considered to have about as much value as a donkey or an ox. When Jesus entered the scene, he introduced new understandings of gender roles and leadership. Through a series of relationships and encounters with both men and women, Jesus shifted the paradigm of true leadership by demonstrating redemption, inclusion, empowerment, and servanthood in how he treated others. While religious teachers—Pharisees, Sadducees, and the like—often took great pride in their ability to lead by superiority, Jesus interrupted this line of thinking with statements like, "whoever wants to be first must be slave of all" (Mark 10:44 NIV). He disrupted the leadership status quo by selecting untrained, flawed disciples and commissioning them to follow him as his protégés.

While religious culture during Jesus' time dictated that only the best and brightest could qualify to study under notable rabbis,

> Jesus went against the grain and developed those that none considered capable of leadership.

Jesus went against the grain and developed those that none considered capable of leadership. He selected tax collectors and spent time around noted sinners, teaching and developing them in his ways (Mark 2:14–16). He developed them through a series of life events that often included the testing of their faith and the proving of their devotion. As their leader, Jesus taught them, directly and indirectly, through the life he lived before them. When they were ready, he empowered them to go out in his name, bearing his reputation, and operating in his power (Luke 9:1–6). In so doing, Jesus set a new standard that was contrary to that of the world. He redeemed those whom society disqualified and developed them for leadership in the kingdom of God.

With both men and women, Jesus took the time to call and equip those who would lead his church. He was also intentional in selecting and developing women as disciples and followers of his way. He encouraged them to give, serve, and minister wherever there was a need. He empowered them to minister to others as he did for the woman at the well (John 4) and encouraged them to speak up, as he did for the woman who touched the hem of his garment (Mark 5:25–34). He developed them by creating a space for them at his feet, as he did for Mary, sister of Lazarus (Luke 10:38–42), and redeemed their reputations, as he did for the woman caught in the act of adultery (John 8:1–11). Wherever he went, Jesus selected women as examples of God's will for the church and as models of leading in faith and conviction. Whether directly or indirectly stated, it is clear that Jesus had a heart for women and was not shy about including them in His plan for the kingdom and for the church. Women in Jesus' day became some of the main targets of God's ministry through Christ to turn upside down the ways of the world.

Consider Mary, for example. In his telling of the Gospel story, Luke shows the liberating power of Jesus making room for women to serve in any capacity, and he proved it by beginning his account with two women: Elizabeth and Mary. Through his Gospel, Luke revealed the details about the miraculous birth, in which Mary and Elizabeth are the focal points of faith while their men, Joseph and Zechariah, are left in doubt and disbelief. Jesus could have come to earth in so many different ways, but he chose to come through a humble, seemingly insignificant woman. Through his birth, Jesus redeemed Mary and gave her a place in history that she could not merit.

Mary's attributes of faith, humility, and availability become core traits of servant leadership for men and women who desire to follow Christ. In addition, God's choice of her in the lineage as the sole carrier of the Son of God underscores the role of women in God's redemptive plan for the world. Women can bring life to God's Word! She exemplifies the ways in which women, and especially mothers, are uniquely equipped to serve the church in ministry and leadership.

As an unlikely hero, Mary appeals to the heart and soul of women who seek to be developed for church leadership. She is a young girl of low estate, subject to judgment and ridicule because of her pregnancy predicament, and yet God uses these very things to elevate and favor her above others. Although we do not know the details of her childhood, we know that God prepared her for what she was called to do, not least through the godly companionship of another woman, Elizabeth, herself unexpectedly pregnant. Though it is not clear what happened in her life to make her ready for this amazing task, it is obvious that God made her ready to be the very first carrier of the Word of God. In a way, we could say that Mary was the world's first preacher.

Throughout the gospels, there are countless examples of women leaders developed and used by God, whose experiences also resonate with the lives and experiences of women in ministry today. Much can be said about John's depiction of the Woman at the Well whose cataclysmic encounter with Christ changed an entire village (John 4); or Matthew and Mark's Syrophœnician woman whose sharp wit and determination brought healing to her daughter and the good news of salvation for Gentiles (Matthew 15:21–28 and Mark 7:25–30). From independent sisters like Mary and Martha (Luke 10:38–42) to the named and unnamed women who traveled with the disciples (Luke 8:1–3), the Gospels bloom with evidence of God's desire and plan to develop women as followers of Christ and leaders in ministry. They give all of us women examples of what a life with Christ can look like for the church and they provide proof of the impact of women's leadership for anyone willing to surrender to God's purpose for the kingdom on earth.

Life Application

It is clear from scripture that Jesus allowed and even invited women to participate in his work. He affirmed their importance and encouraged them, along with men, to go and make disciples. There weren't any focused leadership development classes or degree programs for these believers, but we can be sure that Jesus developed every single person that he called. How did he do that, you ask? The answer is simple: *by spending time with them.* Whenever Jesus spent time with his followers, he was investing in their lives. By speaking his word, understanding their situations, and guiding them with his life, he equipped them to carry out his ministry long after he was gone. Every single day of his active ministry, Jesus taught those who would hear, both men and women, the timeless principles of God.

He taught them how to live and how to worship, how to love and serve others, how to act justly and with mercy, and how to prepare for the world to come.

In the same way that he did for the men and women in the Bible, Jesus still calls and develops women as leaders today. He still wants to spend time with us—with you. By investing his word in our lives and leading us by the power of the Holy Spirit, Jesus intentionally equips us for the work of ministry to the world. The same principles of scripture that were cultivated through Jesus' interaction with women can be applied to our lives today.

From Mary, Mother of Jesus, we develop our humility.

From the woman at the well, we develop our courage to face the world.

From Mary and Martha, we learn meditation and service.

From the Syrophoenician woman, we learn boldness and faith.

From Joanna, Suzanna, and the unnamed women who followed Christ, we learn to give God whatever we've got.

The fact that Jesus spent time with women, women whom many people deemed as less than others, shows that he invested himself in them for a greater purpose. With just three years of earthly ministry, Jesus had no time to waste. Every interaction was intentional. Every encounter was designed to grow and to teach someone.

The same principles are true for us today. First, *the greatest step of leadership development comes from our time with the Lord.* The more we spend time with Jesus, the more of himself he invests in us. When we spend time through the disciplines of the Spirit (prayer, meditation, silence, study, and more), we establish a foundation that is critical for any aspect of ministry leadership. Without this foundation, we run the risk of ministry flowing out of our "doing for God" rather than our "being with God." Perhaps this is what God was doing in my early years of leading Bible study. While I was spending time with God in an empty space, God was preparing me to lead a group of thirty women the following year, all willing to receive what God had invested in me. What may feel like empty space in your life right now may actually be an invitation to spend more time with Jesus.

The second major principle that we can glean from Jesus and the women in the Gospels is that *God can use every part of your life as preparation for leadership.* What stands out the most about the women called to follow Christ is the fact that many of them had known issues that would have prevented them from coming to Jesus, let alone daring to speak to him in public. Not only did Jesus still choose to interact with them, but he also did not allow what had happened to them to stop his ministry through them.

> God can use every part of your life as preparation for leadership.

Think about the woman at the well. Jesus easily could have said that there were too many men in her past (and present) for her to represent him in any substantial way. I'm sure there were many other women Jesus could have chosen to encounter. And yet, because he ministered to her, she literally dropped everything to tell others about him. We can even speculate that she told her men about this new man that had changed her life. While she may have been used to talking to people in one way (to get something), her encounter with Christ motivated her to talk to people in a new way (to give something). Perhaps this is what led them to say, "It is no longer because of what you said that we believe, for we have heard for ourselves, and we know that this is indeed the Savior of the world" (John 4:42 ESV).

It brings me great joy to know that God can use every part of our lives, even the parts we think are unworthy, as preparation for ministry. I've even heard someone say that God will turn your misery into your ministry. That was certainly true for many of the women in the Bible. Because of their encounters with Christ, women found their troubles turned into testimonies, their ability to seduce turned into an aptitude to serve, and their points of shame turned into shouts of praise! These women teach us that there is no part of your life that can't be turned around for God's good purpose and ministry.

For those whose lives were less-than-perfect (that'd be all of us, right?), Jesus reminds us that he can turn those things around for his good. For those whose lives seem uneventful or insignificant, he lets us know that he can make every moment matter in the journey to becoming a good leader. Never take for granted the small moments that God brings into our lives. As Mary Magdalene would tell us, you never know when a moment of worship may be preparation for a moment to witness to Christ in a brand-new way. Many of the gospels are thought to point to Mary Magdalene as being the only one who risked her dignity and possibly her life savings to worship Jesus with her perfumed oil (Matthew 26:6–13, Mark 14:3–9, Luke 7:36–50 and John 12:1–8). She invested this one moment in time to honor Jesus while he lived and he boldly declared that she would never be forgotten. As a result, all four gospels also mention Mary as being among the women who first noticed that the tomb where Jesus had been buried was empty. Her passion for Jesus allowed her to witness him in a new way: risen, resurrected, and alive! She then became a carrier of the gospel by telling the other disciples this good news that Jesus had been raised from the dead.

While some people may think that Mary was not a leader in a significant way, she demonstrates for us that God can use every moment to prepare us for ministry leadership in every way. Leadership can take on many forms. Some women may be called to minister in systems that may never recognize their true capacity as pastoral leaders. Others may be called to create their own systems in order to lead and pastor without hindrance. Regardless of your calling, our scriptures testify that every single one is necessary and important to God. Women who serve as pastors cannot look down on those who are evangelists. Women who serve as deaconesses cannot despise or discredit those who serve as deacons. For every role, God prepares us all and uses every part of our lives to make a difference in ministry. Know that the God into whose service you are called will develop you with every gift necessary for your success.

As you consider your own process of development as a ministry leader, take a few moments to answer the following questions:

1. What is God doing in your life right now to prepare you to be a better leader?

2. When was the last time you spent time with the Lord? If it has been a while, when will you start again?

3. Think about your life. What stands out as a leadership development moment from God?

4. When you read about the women in the gospels, with which women do you connect most and why?

Summary

Jesus wants to develop you for your calling. He invites you into an intimate relationship with him, one that can redeem you and transform you into the leader he calls you to be. Our Scriptures affirm repeatedly that God equips those whom God calls and prepares them for all that they are called to do. Jesus called you and therefore he will develop you, so that through you the world will catch a glimpse of God's glory, justice, mercy, and love.

Jesus, thank you for loving me enough to develop me for ministry. Thank you for using every moment and redeeming every part of my past to be used for your glory. Help me to make the most of my time with you. Make me as notable as the women in your Word so that others may see and give you glory and praise. I believe that you are maturing me and I can't wait to see what you have in store for me next! Amen.

3

The Challenge and Charge of Women in Church Leadership

The landscape of leadership for women changes daily as women in leadership become less of an anomaly and more commonplace. Across the globe, women are taking on more high-profile leadership positions as senior executives, presidents, board chairs, and, yes, pastors. Yet, having more women in leadership does not necessarily mean that the challenges of leadership are completely resolved. In fact, most women, in both secular and sacred vocations, would agree that there are still significant challenges that come with serving in leadership.

Going into leadership with a simple love of God will take you far. Going into leadership with your eyes wide open to the challenges will help you soar. Being a person who refuses to allow the challenges to become barriers to success will strengthen the entire Body of Christ. In short, if we can equip women to overcome the challenges of ministry leadership today, we will help to shape an even better leadership environment for the women of tomorrow.

Common Challenges

No ministry context is the same and every person's experience is unique. At the same time, there are still some challenges that seem to be universal for women in the world and in the church. The following stories are compilations of a variety of real experiences of women in ministry that I hope will not only educate you about the realities, but spur you on to do your part in changing them.

Sexism

Every Sunday, the church's ministers gathered in the pastor's office to pray before services began. Being new in ministry, it was an opportunity that Amanda took seriously, seeking God for the lives that would be changed through the worship experience that day. She was grateful to have other women on the staff because while she respected her pastor, there was something about him that made her feel a little uneasy. Once, after praying and before entering the sanctuary, the pastor pulled her aside to say that he liked her skirt. She debated that morning about whether or not the skirt was too short, but decided to wear it, since it fell below the knee. When she asked him if the skirt was inappropriate, he replied, "No, I just like the way it looks on you." From that day on, she vowed never to be in a position where she was alone with him.

Sarah loved to preach. When she preached, when she surrendered herself to the power of the Holy Spirit, she discovered a new side of herself: a bolder, stronger self. One October, after preaching a three-night revival, a gentleman stood in line to shake her hand only to tell her, "I would hate to be your husband. The way you preach, you would win every argument."

In Rosa's church, the pastor's office felt like miles away from the ladies' room. In order to go from one to the other, she literally had to walk through the sanctuary, which would always cause a disturbance if meetings were taking place. Since Rosa was the first woman pastor of the church, she felt it was important for the elders to understand this challenge and consider making adjustments so that she could have a restroom closer to her office. When she raised her concern, they told her, "A change like that is too expensive. You'll just have to accept that life isn't always 'lady-pastor' friendly."

Ageism

Bertha was delighted when she passed her ordination exams. It had been years since she was in school, but, by God's grace, she was able to move forward in her process. She submitted her information for a church opening knowing it was a perfect fit for her skill set. She nearly fainted when she was invited to interview! They requested to do the interview by videoconference. Although it took her two days, thanks to some guidance from her son she figured everything out and got all of the technology in place. After two short questions, the board proceeded to ask about her age, something that is illegal but nonetheless commonplace. As a second-career minister, she knew that she was older than the typical candidate. Her seminary colleagues often commented that she reminded them of their grandmothers. When she shared her age, her interview committee launched into a series of questions about why a person her age would consider this kind of work. At the conclusion of the interview, one of the women in the room suggested that Bertha find work "better suited for where she was in life" instead of applying for a role that demanded innovation and intensity.

Sakenah first joined her church as a college student. Everyone knew she was gifted and she served in nearly every capacity with excellence. After graduation from seminary, she was offered the youth minister position and she was thrilled! She became the youngest staff person in the history of the church. For Sakenah, the people she called colleagues were as old as and even older than her parents, a fact that they reminded her of constantly by calling her "kiddo" or "baby girl." Whenever she brought new ideas to the table, she would hear snide comments like, "She's still wet behind the ears" or "Let's see if she thinks the same way when she grows up." When it was time for the Christmas bonus, she learned that hers was significantly less than others'. When she approached her boss about it, he simply stated that it was a matter of priorities and other ministers with families had greater need than she did. Besides, since she lived at home, he was sure her parents would take care of her Christmas gifts.

Bias against Singleness, Motherhood, and Marriage

"You know that if you become a minister, you might be single for the rest of your life, right?" Jennifer's dad meant well, but he couldn't get over the fact that his only daughter was going into ministry. To him, singleness meant no grandchildren to spoil and no son-in-law to call his own. It meant that his legacy would end with his only child and he could not stand that thought. Ministry would end his dreams. He wanted her to know what she was walking into. Jennifer had been very clear about her calling. Yet, deep down she now began to wonder whether or not single people would be able to advance in ministry. She heard one pastor say, "My ministry didn't really take off until I got married. That's why we don't hire single ministers in our church." At her home church, she learned to smile and remain silent as everyone talked about their kids and spouses and made jokes that she didn't have to worry about "real life." Having to wrestle with these realities, she could not fight the feeling that she could very well be husbandless *and* churchless for a very long time.

Consider Lori, a married new mother and nonprofit executive. Lori's revelation came while using her breast pump in the janitor's closet for the third time that day. Why should an executive for a Christian nonprofit have to hide the fact that

> "My ministry didn't really take off until I got married. That's why we don't hire single ministers in our church."

she's a breastfeeding mom? Everyone knew that she had just had a baby and she was grateful to be able to provide for her child in this way. And yet, the staff preferred that she not talk about it so that she wouldn't be "a stumbling block" for those who did not understand. When she requested that the Board of Directors create a space for her to pump and feed her child, since her office was not private, they replied that it would cost too much money. Besides, their staff was too small to have to adhere to the Family Medical Leave Act, they said, and she should consider other ways of "meeting her personal needs."

Annisa loved the fact that her husband was in ministry. As a clergy couple, they had so much to share with each other and they counted it a blessing that they both understood the challenges of ministry life. They went to school at the same time and her husband always applauded the fact that she got better grades than he did. When she went on to get her doctoral degree, he was in the front row, cheering loudly as she crossed the stage. Although they served at different churches, they supported each other and she always made sure to answer her phone whenever he called.

This was the case when she was in a meeting with the church's executive team and her husband called. They were making decisions about the church calendar when she stepped out to make sure he was okay. When she returned to the meeting, one of the people in the room made a joke that she must have been getting her husband's permission to approve the calendar. She laughed it off and corrected them. At the end of the meeting, one of the staff members walked her out. He cautioned her against always taking her husband's call, saying, "People already think that he makes the decisions for you. It's best if you don't give them any room to believe that's true."

Projection

Sasha was proud of her accomplishments in women's ministry. Serving women was what she loved and she looked forward to the Bible studies she led each week. During their study of women in the Bible, she always found ways to make each character applicable to everyone there. One night after Bible study, one of the new women in the group asked to speak with her. She said that she'd been to lots of women's Bible studies and tonight was one of the worst she had experienced. Sasha was shocked. From her perspective, people loved the teaching and many even said so as they left. She continued listening and asked a few probing questions to get at the heart of the complaint. After about thirty minutes of listening, Sasha had a gut feeling that it wasn't the teaching that the woman didn't like, but her. The next day, one of her leaders called to find out about the conversation. When Sasha shared the details, her leader stated that this was the same woman who shared with her small group that a family member had abused her. At the time, the woman had tried to tell her mother, but her mother had not believed her. Turns out her mother was a women's ministry leader and Bible study teacher too.

Vickie was a counselor to her core. Even in grade school, she found herself mediating between friends, talking peers out of negative behaviors, and listening when others walked away. She always knew that she would go into counseling, and after she committed her life to Christ she knew that her calling would lead her to start a Christian counseling ministry. For years, she counseled married couples together, but in one particular case, the couple could never seem to come at the same time. Most of the time, the wife showed up without her husband and his presence seemed sporadic at best. When Vickie finally asked what was going on, the wife shared that because Vickie resembled his ex-wife, her husband could not look at her without thinking about all of the bad experiences he had had in the past.

Jealousy

JoAnn was smart, attractive, likeable, and had a great sense of humor. She loved being around people and it showed in all that she said and did. As the associate pastor of her church, she was the proxy for the pastor and gladly welcomed people that he did not have time to see. While the pastor was on sabbatical, JoAnn was instructed to take on all of his meetings with congregants so that there would be no hiatus in the pastoral care offered. One such meeting was with one of the lay ministers named Marsha. JoAnn went out of her way to keep her appointments with Marsha and even recognized her as one of the most faithful leaders during worship one Sunday. Yet, despite all of her efforts, Marsha responded to JoAnn rudely. When JoAnn got up to preach, Marsha would walk out or turn the other way. When they saw each other in the hallway, Marsha would walk in the opposite direction. One day, JoAnn's pastor called from vacation to find out how things were going. He indicated that he had received a letter from Marsha detailing all that JoAnn was doing wrong. It was even signed by six other people in the congregation. When JoAnn probed a little further, she learned that Marsha had been one of the finalists for JoAnn's role, but did not get the job.

Patricia was hesitant to apply for the chaplaincy position. She knew that it would be demanding, but she could not resist an opportunity to serve at her alma mater. After submitting her application, a friend from the university told her that she was the only woman among four men that had made it to the final round. Patricia prayed that God would open a door and believed that however things worked out would be for her good. In her interview, she made clear what her vision would be for students on campus and brought references from existing faculty and students from her church. Before she left the interview, they offered her the position as the best qualified for the job. As she was getting into her car, she saw the other candidates talking in a small group. She couldn't hear everything, except for this statement: "She got the job only because she's a woman."

Biblical Observations

Let's face it: life is full of such complexities and challenges. Knowing that they will come is half of the battle; the other half is knowing how to handle them. Queen Esther was a leader who overcame a series of challenges. Through her, God gives us a wonderful example of how God can take what works against us and use it to work for our good.

Esther had so much working against her. As an Israelite in Persia, she came from people that had been exiled from their homeland and forced to dwell among foreign nations. Esther was one of the many who were considered to be second-class citizens, if they were even citizens at all. Her people had experienced loss in a deep sense, having been uprooted from everything that was familiar and sacred to them.

Not only was Esther part of a people who experienced challenges, but she had personal challenges as well. The Bible says that she had neither mother nor father, for both had passed away, leaving her as an orphan (Esther 2:7). She barely remembered what her mother and father looked like because they died when she was just a baby. Although she was adopted by her cousin Mordecai, she never had the privilege of knowing her real parents; parents that knew the date and time of her birth and exactly which side of the family her unique features came from. Yes, Esther experienced challenges in a variety of ways.

But, it seems that people didn't care about Esther's people or the way that she was raised. At least the narrator of our story didn't. It seems that no one was interested in her struggles as a young Jewish woman or the fact that her real name, Hadassah, meant myrtle in her native Hebrew tongue. No, it seems that what was most important to our story was what could be seen on the outside and that's precisely what caused her to be taken away from her home: her beauty. It was her beauty that led the king's men to her house that day. It was her beauty that caused them to herd her off with other women, knowing that she may never again see, smell, touch, or hear what was familiar to her.

Esther struggled in ways that we as modern Western readers may never understand. In a land that did not consider her desires or her will as important to be remembered, Esther struggled to survive under desperate circumstances. And yet, just when it seemed like things couldn't get any worse, they certainly did. It was not enough that she was exiled. It was not enough that she was orphaned. It was not enough that she was taken from her home. On top of all that she had to keep a secret, the secret of her heritage and her people. Her people represented not only her cultural identity but her religious identity as well. Mordecai, as the voice of wisdom, told her to hide her sacred readings. He advised her not to betray her dialect or her love of things from home. Therefore Esther, having been exiled and thrown into the anonymous crowd of beautiful women, was forced to abandon everything that could have identified who she was.

Life Application

How did Esther overcome the challenges she faced to succeed in leadership? For one, *Esther never forgot who she was.* Although Mordecai told her to keep her Jewish identity a secret, she never forgot that she was part of a people who were chosen by God. Because her family lived according to the Law of Moses, Esther was familiar with the stories of how God brought them out of Egypt. She knew about how God delivered the Jews from a series of dangers and carried them through times that seemed impossible to bear. While the name of God is nowhere in the book of Esther, the hand of God is evident with every move she made.

In order to overcome the challenges of leadership, you must never forget who you are. There will be systems that try to break you. There will be people who try to tear you down. You may even have friends who abandon you on your way to becoming who God calls you to be. No matter what happens around you, never ever forget who God made you to be. When others fight to "keep you in your place," remember the scriptures that affirm your place is with God. The Word tells you that you are "fearfully and wonderfully made" (Psalm 139:14). Like Esther, you are being prepared for leadership "for such a time as this," and there are people whom God wants to bless through you

(Esther 4:14). You are a child of the King, a woman of faith, a successful leader—and you've only just begun. Never forget who you are in God.

Not only did Esther know who she was, but *she also knew what she had to do.* When faced with the challenge of being a voice for her people, Esther knew that she had to seek God. Look at what she told Mordecai,

> Go, gather together all the Jews who are in Susa, and fast for me. Do not eat or drink for three days, night or day. I and my attendants will fast as you do. When this is done, I will go to the king, even though it is against the law. And if I perish, I perish" (Esther 4:16 NIV).

Esther understood that she could not do this by herself. Her calling would require a community of people praying, fasting, and believing with her for God to intervene. Once she made her decision, she was willing to stick with it, even if it cost her life.

You may be thinking, "I don't always know what to do." But, if you have a relationship with God, you know exactly what to do in every difficult situation.

> Every Christian woman in leadership needs a prayer posse.

You can pray and get a few others to join you. To overcome the challenges of being women in leadership, we have to know that we cannot do this alone. Every Christian woman in leadership needs a prayer posse. You don't need a whole group of people; you just need two or three who love you enough to pray for you. Be willing to invite people into prayer and even fasting in order for you to hear God's voice. Recognize that the call of leadership is too serious and the challenges you face are too hard for you to move forward without godly direction. And when you hear God's voice, be willing to stand on it, no matter what it costs. Strong leaders take risks. Like Esther, you can take a risk knowing that when you follow God, the results are up to God.

Take a moment and think about some of the challenges you have faced or anticipate facing in leadership.

1. Which of these stories of women in pastoral leadership resonates with you the most and why?

2. What has God done in your life already to prepare you for these challenges?

3. What scriptures remind you of who you are in Christ?

4. Who is in your prayer posse? If you don't have one, whom can you invite to pray for you this week? And is there another woman that you can offer to support through regular prayer?

Summary

With all that works against us, you need to know that there is more for you than you could ever imagine. Being a woman in leadership is hard work. It is even harder if you're a minority woman. It takes an internal strength and conviction of faith that only comes from God but that can be strengthened through having a posse of faithful praying women and men. There will be days when you wonder whether you've chosen the right path; days when you feel as if the fight simply isn't worth it at all. But, the good news is that God is for you. God is with you. God has placed you in the right place at the right time and you will succeed! You were made for this!

Lord, I confess that I sometimes get sidetracked by the challenges against me and forget what's most important. With you by my side, I know there is no challenge too great and that together we can overcome anything. Help me to remember who you called me to be and give me strength to do your will. Surround me with people who will pray for me when I need it most. I thank you and I anticipate victory! In Jesus' name. Amen.

SECTION 2

GET SET!

4

Confidence

Insecurity is like acid. One small drop can burn a hole through just about anything, including your success. Ask anyone and they will tell you that an insecure leader will not and cannot go far. A confident leader, on the other hand, has the power to lead others and soar in just about any field. A Christ-centered servant leader who is not only confident in herself but also in God can do anything that she sets her heart to do.

Now, before we get too far in this discussion, let's talk about what confidence is *not*. Confidence is not arrogance. Period. Arrogance comes from people who are overly confident in themselves, which gives very little room for God. A prideful person takes pride in their own work and their own success, without recognizing God as the source of their accomplishments. At times, arrogance and pride are cover-ups for insecurity. Sometimes, people who puff themselves up in one area are trying to keep you from seeing the truth in another area. These are the ones who crush people trying to get to the "top," believing that there's not enough leadership opportunity or exposure to go around. They also believe that they are entitled to the top positions and will destroy anyone in order to get there. Eugene

Peterson's *The Message* Bible says it well: "First pride, then the crash—the bigger the ego, the harder the fall" (Proverbs 16:18). If you don't like crashing, now is a good time to root your confidence in the right place.

Scripture encourages us to place our confidence in God and God alone. Hebrews 10:35 tells us not to throw away our confidence because it will be rewarded at the right time. For leaders, godly confidence can lead people closer to God and strengthen faith, both theirs and yours. Whenever you accept the challenge of trusting God and encourage others to do the same, you will find that God will come through in ways you never imagined. The more you trust God, the more confident you become. The more confident you become in God, the more God can do in and through you.

> **The more you trust God, the more confident you become.**

The Dangers of Insecurity

Terry had a challenging childhood. Her mother was an alcoholic and her father left when she was an infant. She was the youngest of five siblings, but most of them were either in jail, on drugs, or on their way there. If it had not been for her grandmother teaching her about God when she was just three years old, Terry knew that she would not be alive.

Terry loved her grandmother and being with her became the only reprieve from a sad and depressing family life. They went to church every Sunday and Wednesday together, praying, singing, and believing that God could make a difference in their family. Terry's grandmother was her life and when she passed away, Terry fell into a deep depression. She was in high school and began to rebel from God and follow the wayward habits of her brothers and sisters. She was angry with God and could not believe that God would do something so cruel as to take the one person who looked after her.

By God's grace, Terry was accepted into college, but that did not change her behaviors. After a series of promiscuous relationships along with alcohol and drug abuse, she finally hit a wall one night. She woke up in a strange place and heard her grandmother calling out to her. Although she was hung over, she felt surrounded by God's presence. In that moment, she heard a voice saying, "You were made for more." That was the beginning of her transition out of darkness and into the light of God. She let go of damaging relationships, gave up every substance that brought her down, and changed her life around. Things were so dramatic that even her professors began to notice. God was making a difference in her life.

A few years later, Terry found herself in the least likely place: serving as a youth minister in a church. She was gifted, knowledgeable, spirit-filled, and she loved what she did. Yet although everything in her life had turned around, she still felt like that little girl who had been abandoned by the one person who loved her the most. As a result, she regularly second-guessed her decisions, making her look uncertain to the volunteers that followed her. She was haunted by her past and turned down opportunities all the time, feeling as if she wasn't good enough for bigger things. Even the young people noticed Terry's lack of confidence. As a result, rather than talking to her they went to other people on staff for advice, letters of recommendation, and other serious matters. To them, she was like one of their peers with the same problems they had. Despite the fact that she was gifted for leadership, Terry never felt strong enough, good enough, pure enough, or worthy enough to serve others.

Insecurity can come from many places and shows up in many different ways. Leaders that lack confidence:

1. Have trouble making decisions or second-guess the ones they make

2. Overcompensate on the job

3. Take on other people's baggage

4. Always feel the need to prove their worth

5. Kiss up to people that they perceive are on the top

6. Struggle to do what they know is right

7. Remain silent in meetings, even when they have something good to say

8. Act as if they don't belong

9. Accept less than desirable actions/pay/treatment because they think they don't deserve more; and most alarmingly they

10. Live beneath their callings.

These behaviors often leave women frustrated, fearful, and left behind in places where we don't belong. But, here's the good news: if you find yourself exhibiting any of the behaviors above, there is hope for you! With just a mustard seed of faith, God can turn an insecure, self-doubting woman into one who walks in confidence and grace.

Biblical Observations

The fourth chapter of the book of Judges introduces us to two models of confident women leaders: Deborah and Jael. Deborah was a prophetess and judge during a time when the children of Israel were under the reign of Jabin, king of Canaan. She would "sit under the palm tree of Deborah . . . and the children of Israel came up to her for judgment" (Judges 4:5 NKJV). In this role of authority, she could not afford to waiver in her decisions. With people trusting her to hear from God, she had to walk in godly confidence, believing that God would speak to her and through her for the good of the people. We see this demonstrated when she sent for Barak, and told him that the Lord wanted him to take down Sisera, the commander of Jabin's army. In interesting contrast to Deborah's godly confidence, Barak showed his lack of confidence and refused to go without her. Although God had spoken of his success, Barak was not confident that it would happen without Deborah as his support. She told him that she would go, but she also said, "the honor will not be yours, for the LORD will deliver Sisera into the hands of a woman" (Judges 4:9 NIV). At the time, we assume Deborah is speaking about herself, but God had another woman in mind.

Jael is presented as a simple housewife of her time. She was keeping the tent, presumably while her husband was away at war, when the enemy soldier Sisera came to her for refuge. Had she been insecure, she would have called someone else to help her or sounded an alarm that the enemy was in her tent. Had she wavered, she may have let him get away. And had she second-guessed her own abilities to handle the situation, she would have missed a major opportunity. But she didn't waver and if she second-guessed herself, she did not let it keep her from doing what she needed to do. The Bible states that after she gave him milk to drink, Jael "picked up a tent peg and a hammer and went quietly to [Sisera] while he lay fast asleep, exhausted. She drove the peg through his temple into the ground, and he died" (Judges 4:21 NIV). Then, when Barak came looking for him, she stood boldly outside her tent and told him that she knew exactly where the enemy was. God used Jael to fulfill Deborah's prophecy that Sisera would die at the hand of a woman.

Life Application

God used both Deborah and Jael to redeem Israel. They were bold women who trusted themselves and God to fulfill a promise. In the same way, God can use you to do great things for the Kingdom when you walk in confidence. So, how can you build Godly confidence? Here are a few ways that you can do starting today:

1. Trust your gifts. Both Deborah and Jael were gifted in different ways. Deborah was gifted to prophesy and judge the people. Because she trusted her gifts and was not afraid to operate in them, she stands in history as the first female judge and one of many that God used to deliver the people. Jael was also gifted—at keeping tents. While she was not granted the opportunity to serve as publicly as Deborah, she simply used what she had to get the job done. She trusted her tent-making skills and used them as a weapon against the enemy. You and I can go far when we trust the gifts we have been given. Be confident in the fact that you've been given the right gifts for the right role at the right time.

> **Be confident in the fact that you've been given the right gifts for the right role at the right time.**

2. Practice, practice, practice. While the Bible does not say it explicitly, we can assume that Deborah had some practice with judging the people. She may not have been very confident when she first started, but the more she served, the better she became. Even when the assignment seemed small, like it may have felt for Jael when she used the tent peg, the impact was significant. The more she practiced hearing God's voice, the stronger her confidence became. The same is true today. The more practice you can get operating in your gifts, the more confident you will become. Look for opportunities to serve God and do not despise the small things. Take every class, internship, volunteer assignment, new responsibility, and staff opening you can find when you start out. Find things you're good at and do them for the glory of God. You'll find that you can build your resumé and your confidence at the same time.

3. Sing your own song. Judges chapter five records a victory song that Deborah and Barak sang about all that God had done through them. They sang of God's faithfulness and also of Deborah's power. Their voices rang out with news of God's blessings and also the blessedness of Jael. They were not afraid to tell the world what God had done and to remind themselves of the part they had played. Sometimes, you have to learn to sing your own song. Don't wait for people to celebrate your accomplishments. Make your own affirmations about what God has done through you. Write notes to yourself and stick them on the door. Post scriptures of affirmation that remind you of who God has called you to be. Celebrate what God does through you and you will build your confidence on a firm foundation.

4. Welcome feedback. Neither of the women operated in isolation. As a prophet, Deborah was subject to the judgment of God and to the community she served for all that she said. Jael took a major risk when she invited Barak into her tent to see the dead solider. Both women could have been subject to serious criticism, as any leader will be. So instead of running from your critics, instead of being defensive, invite their feedback. Welcome feedback as a gift and keep the pieces of advice that will help you to grow. Confidence comes from being aware of how you are perceived and from being unafraid to grow from what others say.

The key to each of these steps is simple: take time to get to know yourself. Don't be afraid or ashamed of who God made you to be. As you find out who you are and as you operate out of that awareness, God will increase your confidence and allow you to lead people with strength and power.

As you work to grow your confidence, think about the following questions:

1. What have you accomplished so far that makes you proud?
2. How does insecurity show up for you?
3. When do you feel the most confident? Least?
4. What is God calling you to do today to help build your confidence?

Summary

None of us is confident all of the time. As leaders, we will have doubts and insecurities. We may second-guess ourselves from time to time. Yet the Bible is clear that we should never allow these things to keep us from being confident leaders in God. As we grow in our gifts through practice, celebration, and feedback, we will discover that we are capable of so much more. We can have confidence in ourselves when we learn to trust that God is working in and through us for good.

God, thank you for reminding me that you are up to something good in my life. I believe, in spite of my weaknesses, that I am a strong leader. I am capable of great things and I am good at what I do. When people see my work, they marvel at the hand of God on my life. I am not egotistical or conceited. I am confident in you. Help me to trust and honor you every step of the way. Amen.

5

Your Love Life

I started in full-time ministry as a single woman. At least once a week, some random person felt it was important for me to know that I may never get married.

"You do know that very few men would want to marry a preacher, right?"

"I hope you're not planning to pastor because then you'll *never* get married!"

"Are you a minister? Does that mean that you're like a nun?"

I even had a wedding planner tell me that she'd love to plan my wedding someday, but that frankly it was unlikely that I'd ever walk down the aisle.

After hearing this over and over again, I started to buy into the talk. I started thinking that because I chose to follow God in ministry, I must also have chosen to sacrifice my love life for the Lord. Slowly, I started believing that my calling to ministry was synonymous with a call to eternal singleness. While I knew this was true for some women, I wrestled with whether it was true for me. I stopped looking at potential suitors and started throwing my whole life into ministry. I slept with a notepad next to my bed so that I could write down new ministry ideas. I turned down opportunities to hang out with friends because

I had ministry events that took place at night. In fact, I started planning more events on Friday and Saturday nights because I figured that if I didn't have plans as a single Christian, no one else did either. Unfortunately, ministry became my cover and my cave. I hid myself in ministry so that I would not have to think about the fact that I was single.

On the outside, I was proud to make such a significant step for God. Yet, on the inside, I struggled with the fact that I did eventually want to get married. I allowed other people to make me believe that being a minister meant that I was somehow undesirable or unattractive. I had been in a number of conversations with potential dates, only to have the conversation end abruptly after they found out what I did for a living. After that, I started "twisting the truth" about my vocation when men would ask. If the conversation was a good one, I'd say that I was a counselor or teacher or, my personal favorite, a commodities broker. I felt justified because I was technically all of these things— just in a church, with people, as a minister. Small details, right?

After years of such mind games and terrible dates, I finally settled with God. Whether single or married, I was called to serve the Lord *and* to have a love life. I started "Operation Get-A-Life" to break me out of this pattern of using ministry to cover the pain of singleness. I started allowing and even inviting other leaders to take on weekend events so that I could get out and do something beyond the church. I joined a salsa dance class, went white-water rafting, read really good books, and went on vacation. Yes, I was a single minister, but I started to enjoy my life. It wasn't the same kind of satisfaction I wanted to have from marriage, but it forced me to realize something critically important: God had called me to love the life I had been given.

More than Marriage

In 2010, I married my best friend, Mark Martin. We had a beautiful wedding and I am blessed to be with someone who knows exactly who I am and still sees himself called to be with me in life and ministry. While marriage meant I was done with crazy comments about being a single minister, I was now open to a brand-new set of biases. Instead of comments about my singleness, I now received unsolicited comments and advice about my marriage and children.

"I can tell who wears the pants in your house by the way you preach."

"Be careful not to take too many late meetings. There are always women in the church that want to bring him a casserole."

"Your husband is such a good man to marry a minister."

After the birth of our second child, one sincere woman even pulled me aside to share that God told her that I should consider quitting or going part-time to take care of my family. After all, my children needed their mommy more than the church needed me as a minister.

These and other comments planted seeds of doubt within me again. Was I sure that God could use wives and mothers in pastoral leadership? Would I have to fight harder to keep my marriage because I was in ministry? And worst of all, would my children grow up to resent me because of my calling? After some time of struggle, I finally realized the truth: these doubts and questions come from an outdated model of ministry. The assumption was that ministry meant giving your life to others at the expense of your home and family. It meant taking calls at the dinner table, choosing to lead funerals instead of going on vacation, and missing your child's program to teach a Bible study. In the old model, being in a position of leadership within the church meant not sharing important times with your family or not spending intimate time with your spouse. While it may be easy for a man to make these exceptions, the old model assumed that it was unacceptable for a wife or mother to play this role.

But as a woman in ministry, I never wanted the witness of my marriage to send the message that you cannot be a leader and have a healthy marriage. On the contrary, God taught me something unique: wives who are called to ministry are called to healthy marriages as the primary witness of God's ministry. Yes, you can be an effective Christian leader *and* an amazing wife at the same time! The way to do it is to create new models of ministry. While there are certainly times in any vocation at which individuals will need to make sacrifices, these occurrences can be occasional and do not have to be the rule. By setting boundaries with the church, I found that I could lead from a healthier place with my family and set a better example for others on my team. For example, when I made decisions based on how they impacted my family, that gave others permission to put their families first as well. In the early stages, I was nervous that my model would send the message that it was okay for others to slack off. On the contrary, I was able to create an environment where people worked diligently because they knew that I cared not only about what they did but also about who they were.

This new understanding of ministry for me was not easy. It required disappointing some important people and constantly restating my values to everyone in my life, including myself. There are still times when I struggle and wonder if I'm effective in any area. Yet, in the midst of it all, God brings confirmation that a new leadership model can bring life to my family and health to the church at the same time.

> Wives who are called to ministry are called to healthy marriages as the primary witness of God's ministry.

Biblical Observations

Proverbs 31 is probably the most widely quoted scripture when it comes to women in ministry. It is a beautiful passage of scripture that describes an amazing woman who seems to have it all and do it all. Unfortunately, it also sets a superwoman standard that can make any woman feel like an underachiever. According to the scripture, this woman:

- Makes her husband happy every single day

- Rewards him with good things every single day
- Selects fabrics and makes clothes for everyone—by hand
- Goes grocery shopping and then wakes before the sun comes up to cook food for the entire household
- Has the skill set and money to assess land, buy it, and plant a vineyard
- Has an amazing body with nice biceps
- Makes good money and never sleeps
- Is not afraid of working with her hands
- Gives to the poor and those in need
- Has no fear for cold weather because everyone in her house wears the layers of clothes she made—by hand
- Makes her own bed sheets and sews her own clothing—by hand
- Sells the clothes and belts she makes and delivers them to local stores
- Is strong and honorable
- Knows how to laugh
- Speaks wisdom and teaches with love
- Manages the activities of the house and never rests
- Is loved by her children, and
- Is praised by her husband.

The best part of this passage is verse 29, which says "Many women are capable, but you surpass them all!" (HCSB). Well, of course she does! This woman is superwoman! She does everything well and everyone loves her. While her husband and children praise her, there is no mention of them *helping* her. She is both a homemaker and a working mom. She is both honored in the world and honored in the home. This woman is everything and we've been taught to strive to be like her.

Life Application

Newsflash: the Proverbs 31 woman does exist today, just differently. Today's superwoman is super because of who she is, not because of what she does. Therefore, we do not have to assess ourselves based on doing everything all the time and doing it well. No one does that. No woman in leadership, no matter how it looks on the outside, can manage every single area in her life. What she can do is strive to be the woman God has called her to be, for the season she's in, with the help of the Holy Spirit, and to the best of her abilities. She can also build a nice-sized village of people to help fill in the spaces. Even the Proverbs 31 woman had servants in her household for whom she provided. Whether it's a children's day-care provider, a friend who helps from time to time, or the department store from which she buys ready-made clothes, every superwoman has a super team to help her live out her calling.

With that in mind, here are a few tips for single women in ministry:

1. Get a love life. Yes, that's right! Learn to love the people God has already placed around you. Become the most loving daughter, friend, and sister that you can be. Send Valentine's Day gifts, celebrate birthdays, and cultivate love as often as you can. You have been gifted to love deep and wide. Use that gift to bless others and glorify God.

2. Define your own space. Don't let anyone tell you how you should be as a single minister. If you want to date, do so in a way that honors God. If you prefer not to date, stand confidently in your decision to serve God in this way. You are in a unique position that very few will understand. Know that God honors where you are and will keep you in this season.

3. Refuse to let ministry be your crutch. It would be a poor witness for people to see you at every Friday night event and every Saturday breakfast. Learn to set boundaries now so that you can exercise self-care. Sleep in. Go out. Enjoy this time. People will only respect your time if you respect it as well.

4. Don't lose hope. If you feel called to marry, don't give up. God knows where you are and God can design the right person for you at the right time. There are plenty of men who would be honored to be a first gentleman! Put your trust in God and serve with grace. In due season, God will give you the desires of your heart (Psalm 37:4).

> No woman in leadership, no matter how it looks on the outside, can manage every single area in her life.

Here are a few tips for wives and mothers in ministry:

1. Keep your love life first. Yes, bring back your sexy side and go on a date with your spouse! Refuse to let ministry cause you to forget your anniversary. Whether your spouse supports you or not, whether your children are saved or not, you are called to minister to them and show God's love to them before all others. While people may love you for what you can do for them, your spouse is the one who loves you for who you are. If healthy ministries come from healthy families, then ask God to show you how to be present for the people who matter most.

2. Define the new normal. Contrary to popular belief, you cannot be all things to all people. Regardless of what others did before you, women can and should introduce new models of leading in ministry. Don't allow yourself to be bound by the expectations of others. Instead, let others see the witness of God working through you to reframe leadership for the next generation. If we do this well, our granddaughters will thank us.

3. Refuse to buy in to the guilt. If there is such a thing as mommy-guilt, then clergy-mommy guilt must be even more intense. It's one thing to have to leave your spouse or kids for a meeting, but it feels worse to leave them for the church during times when families are typically together. It can be challenging to know that Sundays may never be family time for you in the way that they are for others. Before you throw away your collar, ask God to help you discern the source of the guilt. There may be times when the guilt is unnecessary because your spouse is fine and your kids are in good hands. There are other times when the guilt is a sign of something deeper that needs to be dealt with through counseling and support or a shift in your priorities. Once you understand what's really at stake, don't let anyone make you feel guilty for the choices you've made. Trust that God knew who you were when God called you.

4. Let your family find their own places in the church. In the ideal world, your spouse and your children would love being at church with you all the time. They would celebrate extra-long services and jump for joy for weeknight meetings. In the real world, that is probably not the case. Rather than forcing your husband into the men's ministry or cajoling your children into the youth choir, let them find their own spaces. By giving them the freedom to choose for themselves, they can develop their own passion for God that goes beyond you. In some cases, this may even mean giving them the freedom to choose their own place to worship. At the end of the day, do what it takes to help them cultivate their own callings.

Summary

Whether you were single or married, divorced or widowed, with children or without, God knew who you were when God called you. The best thing you can do is to live out your calling by embracing your status and devoting time to self and family care. Navigate the seasons of ministry with discernment and grace, knowing that there will be imbalance from time to time. Yet, as long as the exceptions never become the rule, the people who love you most will thank God for your ministry.

Consider the following questions for your life:

1. What myths and assumptions do you carry about being single or married in ministry?

2. What is your vision for being a healthy single or married woman in ministry?

3. Whom will you have to disappoint in order for this vision to come to pass?

4. What is God calling you to do today to cultivate and prioritize your love life?

Prayer for Single Women as Leaders

God, thank you for reminding me that you care about my love life. You want me to be whole in singleness, not lacking anything. Create the right community around me that will keep me grounded. Help me to cultivate a life beyond ministry that is a witness to how great you are. If it be your will, mold the right person for me and let me be open when they come. I trust you and commit my love life to you. Amen.

Prayer for Married Women as Leaders

Lord, thank you for my spouse. I confess that marriage is hard work, but I thank you for trusting me with it. Tune my heart to my spouse as my first ministry. Allow our love to be a witness to the world about the love you have for your people. Give me the strength to set clear boundaries so that healthy ministry will be the fruit of healthy marriage. Help me to love in a way that honors you daily. Amen.

Prayer for Mothers as Leaders

God, thank you for the gift of children. You have called me to be a steward over their lives and I am grateful for the challenge. Help me to prioritize my tasks in such a way that my children never get my leftovers but always get the best love I can give. Replace the guilt with grace and help me to find even greater joy in serving my family and your kingdom at the same time. Amen.

6

Sacred Space

"It's lonely at the top" describes the reality that greater leadership responsibilities often mean fewer friends. The same is true in ministry. You may have started your journey with a large circle of friends, but once you accept the call to serve God in ministry, your circle becomes a little smaller. Then, when God begins to elevate you into positions of leadership, that small circle is reduced even more. Some women may even tell you that once you start serving as a pastor, director, chaplain, or executive leader, what started as a circle can turn into a short line of one or two people.

This can be a disturbing experience for those who are unprepared. In this regard, ministry can leave you feeling extremely isolated and alone. The situation can be exacerbated by the fact that ministry work often calls you to be surrounded by people who know and love you for what you do. Very few people will know and love you for who you are. Because of these and other unique challenges facing women in ministry, it can feel as if no one understands what you are going through. But, there is a solution: I call it sacred space.

Sacred Space Defined

When I was younger, my sister and I were obsessed with tents. We made them out of anything: blankets, towels, sheets, and even tree branches. The rules for a good tent were simple: only sisters and friends could come in, parents had to stay out, and there must be something sweet to eat inside. Our tents became places of escape, either together or by ourselves. We could create them at any time, in any place, and when we did, we could transform our environments into places of refuge and retreat. I guess one could say we were in the early stages of designing sacred spaces.

Sacred spaces are necessities for anyone called to serve God in ministry. They are the precious times and spaces in our lives that we designate to be "holy ground." Simply put, sacred spaces are the tents we make to encounter the holy. Like rivers of living water in desert lands, God intends sacred spaces to fill and replenish the parched souls of those who serve. With all that we give and all that we pour out, there has to be space for God to restore and revitalize us.

In ministry, there are three areas of sacred spaces that must be defined for good leadership: sacred space with God, sacred space with others, and sacred space with yourself. Like tents, these spaces can be protected based on who can come in, who is kept out, and what sweets can be enjoyed while there.

> Simply put, sacred spaces are the tents we make to encounter the holy.

Sacred Space with God

Sacred space with God is critical for any believer. It is intentional space to be still with the Lord and to enjoy authentic communion with God. Traditionally, we would call this "quiet time." When I was in college, I was taught that the formula for a good quiet time usually involved a song, a passage of scripture or a devotional book, a reflection journal, prayer and more singing, usually in that order. It was a great way to start and allowed me to connect with God in an intentional way. The problem is I began to believe that this was the only way to encounter God's holiness. I became ritualistic about it, and after a few years my quiet time became a task instead of an act of love.

Sacred space with God should not be static, robotic, or formulaic. There is no magic length of time that must be observed or a specific book that must be followed in order for the Holy Spirit to enter. It is simply about creating a space to cultivate intimacy with God and to bring your whole, unfiltered self to the One who loves you most. Sometimes sacred space with God involves cursing, crying, screaming or shouting. Other times, this space is marked by silence and contemplation, making space for God to show up however God desires. No matter what this space looks or feels like, the key is to make sure it becomes part of your daily life.

It is not uncommon for people to serve God without actually taking time to be with God. The pace of life and ministry does not always permit us to stop and be still in God's presence. On top of that, taking time to be with God will always cost us something. It may cost us missing a call or text, turning down an opportunity to be with others, or a chance to get a few other things done. Yes, spending time with God will always be a sacrifice. By turning down other really good things in order to be with God, we offer the sacrifice of our time. In the discipline of sacred space with God, we reaffirm the Lordship of Jesus and allow everything else to fall in line. In this way, ministry and leadership can flow out of loving relationship with God instead of boring obligation. Without this refreshing daily practice, we can miss the voice of the One who called us in the first place.

Sacred Space with Others

In addition to spending time with God, sacred space can be created when we spend time with people who really "get" you and understand what God is doing through you. Every woman leader can feel isolated, but having at least one or two friends who love you for *you* can make all the difference in the world. Unlike regular friendships, sacred spaces with others allow you to share, vent, and confess some of the unique situations of ministry without feeling judged or fixed. These are confidential connections with people who understand the sensitivity of the work to which you are called. They allow you to laugh about awkward moments and cry about challenging times, and they can keep you in check when your faith goes astray. These are probably not the people who always want something from you. You'll have plenty of those connections in ministry and, if you're not careful, relationships like those will leave you feeling empty and dry. Instead, sacred spaces with others should leave you feeling full and whole. They are most often created with lifelong friends, colleagues in ministry, loved ones who understand God's calling, and prayer partners who help to carry you through. While you may not see your sacred community right now, you can believe that it is there. Ask God to reveal the people ordained for this space in your life.

The important thing about sacred spaces with others is to remember that they are necessary for your well-being. Too often, the calling of ministry causes leaders to put relationships on the back burner. Women who serve the church, particularly those with children, can feel as if they don't have time to make or keep friendships. Yet, being real with God requires that we cultivate space to be real with others who genuinely care for who we are. This kind of authentic, trusted community with others requires the same intentionality, effort, and time that we give to ministry. While it may not happen every day or even every week, good leaders will make time for sacred community as a regular part of devotional life.

Sacred Space with Self

Every leader needs time for herself. I'm certain that introverts will wholeheartedly agree while extroverts, like myself, may wonder if this is really necessary at all. Sacred space with self is not indulgent or reclusive. Like other aspects of the sacred life, it is an intentional tent created for you to be you and to care for yourself before caring for others. It is the act of putting on your own oxygen mask before attempting to assist others. For some people, time for yourself involves manicures and pedicures. For others, it may be a walk in the park or a stroll through the mall. Sacred space for self allows you to affirm who you are, with all your weaknesses and strengths, without being swayed by the thoughts of others. It allows you to declare your own worth and care for your own soul with the same care you would give to others.

For women in ministry, it is easy to put everyone before yourself. It's easy to think that we should take care of the needs of others before we tend to our own needs. But good leaders create regular time and space to be by themselves and care for themselves as a witness of their own value. I've heard it said that you teach people how to treat you by how you treat yourself. If we believe the fact that we are made in God's image, then taking care of ourselves should become like any other discipline of the Spirit. This can take on many forms, depending on the level of care we need. For some, self-care means scheduling time to talk to a counselor as an act of caring for our hearts and minds. For others, it means sleeping in or making time to enjoy a favorite treat. No matter what we choose, we can view such care as an act of worship to God. We honor God when we take care of ourselves. This is the intentional act of thanking God for who we are and dedicating time to be a good stewards over our lives.

The Search for Sacred Space

My own search for sacred space is an ongoing journey. So often, I struggled to maintain the regular discipline of settling down to be with God, cultivating sacred community, or taking time for myself. With all of the roles I played as wife, mother, daughter, sister, niece, granddaughter, friend, writer, minister, and so much more, it seemed there was never enough margin in my life to do anything that feels sacred. When I did have moments to commune with God, they often started strong and ended about five minutes later with me falling asleep on my Bible or nodding off in my prayers. Knowing the importance of sacred space, I constantly felt like a failure, incapable of creating space in my life to encounter God in a meaningful way. And then the revelation came: maybe God was not waiting for me to create a special space. Perhaps God would take the mundane spaces in my life and make them sacred for my good.

With this revelation, I began to understand that sacred space was not always about me doing something for God. By God's grace, these spaces were all about God doing something for me. I began to see this truth manifested in my life in some pretty unexpected ways. Once, while giving my toddler a bath, the washing away of dirt made me think about the depth of God's love in washing away my sins. I was overwhelmed with gratitude and began to sing to God as my daughter and I played in the water. It happens frequently in the kitchen. Whether washing dishes or making dinner, God usually finds a way to take my thoughts captive and make them prisoners of Love. Before I know it, God transforms the mundane into holy ground.

I now have countless examples of God transforming common spaces of my life into sacred encounters. By God's grace, I've seen text message conversations with friends transform into foundations for authentic community. I've witnessed my morning coffee runs turn into sacred space just for me. I've even seen how God can take the common task of taking a shower and turn it into sacred worship and praise. While I am nowhere near where I would like to be in this journey to create regular sacred time and space, I am a witness to the fact that God can work with what we have until we get to where we want to be.

Biblical Observations

Elijah was one serious prophet. Through him, God spoke truth that no one else could and demonstrated power that no one else had. With God's strength, he opposed the king and openly challenged false prophets to a game of testing the real God. In one of the most dramatic Biblical showdowns ever, Elijah encouraged 450 prophets of Baal to call on their god while he called on his God to send fire to consume a sacrifice.[1] He watched and waited while they jumped and shouted and cut themselves, hoping that Baal would show up. After giving them an entire day, he then straightened up his altar, laid out the sacrificial bull on the wood and stone, and poured water on it three times! Once it was time, he prayed a two-sentence prayer and God sent fire that not only consumed the offering, but the altar, the stones, the water, and the dust around it. As if that wasn't enough, he then slaughtered all of the false prophets by his own hand, all 450 of them!

But, after all God had done for him and through him, Elijah desperately needed sacred space. His triumphant acts led to death threats and the prophet was afraid. He ran for his life, hoping that God would just allow him to die. He had no one around him, no one to support him, and he probably felt like nothing was sacred anymore. After doing great things for God, Elijah needed God to do something great for him.

Life Application

Sometimes, it takes a monumental moment to make us realize the importance of sacred space. Elijah's story shows us that desperate times call for sacred spaces. In ministry, victorious mountaintop moments are often followed by the sorrow and emptiness of a valley experience. These valleys can come when we are tired or weak or lonely or sad. They can catch us off guard and leave us longing for something sacred when everything around us seems secular. Yet, as God designed spaces of replenishment and perspective for Elijah, God will do the same for all who are chosen to seek and to serve.

In 1 Kings 19, God created sacred space for Elijah by providing food for him to eat. Elijah was tired. He was frustrated.

He wanted to give up and die. But, just when he reached the end of his rope, God gave him food to eat that would strengthen him for the journey ahead. Just as God provided nourishment for Elijah, I believe *God provides sacred space as nourishment for every Christian leader.* Think of sacred space as God's soul food. By designing sacred moments of divine encounters with the Holy Spirit, others, and ourselves, God is indeed feeding our souls. This also means that a life without sacred spaces is a life that is starved of godly nutrition. Live without eating and you'll die a slow and painful death. Choose to make space for the sacred and you'll thrive and be healthy.

> Think of sacred space as God's soul food.

After feeding Elijah, God then created space to speak to him in the silence or in a still, small voice. The Lord had something to say and needed a space to ensure that Elijah would hear it. The good news is that God has something to say to you too! Therefore, *God designs sacred spaces so that we can hear God's voice.* As a leader, there will be times when the only voice you need to hear is God's. At times isolation and loneliness give you the space to hear. Just as God drew Elijah to a cave to speak, God still draws us (sometimes kicking and screaming) into secluded caves just so that we can hear God speak and have space in which to respond. The sacred space becomes the place for God to minister to our unique needs. God wants to meet the needs of those who meet the needs of others.

Once Elijah was fed and ministered to, God gave him something else sacred: sacred relationships with people to help do the work to which he was called. The prophet was instructed to anoint Hazael as king over Syria, Jehu as king over Israel, and Elisha as the prophet who would succeed him. Although Elijah may have felt as if he was alone, God gave clear direction that this mission would no longer be solo. There would be others with the same passion and zeal to make an impact on the nations.

In this journey, *God ordains sacred space to show us our allies.* When people and their needs constantly surround us, it's hard to discern those who are sincerely for us. But, in the sacred moments, God reveals relationships to strengthen us by extending our purpose and mission. These relationships, appointed by God, have the ability to sharpen us "as iron sharpens iron" (Proverbs 27:17 NRSV). They are people who fight the same fight, carry the same values, and share the same pain. When the burdens of ministry seem too much to bear, God will reveal and send allies who will bear them with you. These allies are so sacred and so critical that God must reveal them. Trying to cultivate this kind of community on our own will only lead to frustration and disappointment. Although no relationship is perfect, sacred connections with others draw us closer to God and keep us from short-circuiting our purpose.

In your sacred space with God, take some time to reflect on the following questions:

1. Why do you think finding sacred space is such a challenge for women in leadership?
2. What will it take for you to enjoy sacred space on a regular basis?
3. What relationships has God revealed to form your sacred community?
4. Name two or three things that you can do to take better care of yourself this week.

Summary

The demands of life and ministry can be overwhelming and isolating. You can easily feel as if you're on this journey by yourself. But God has designed sacred spaces to rejuvenate and strengthen every believer, especially leaders. Sacred spaces with God, sacred community with others, and sacred time for yourself all play a role in developing God's purpose and plan for your life. This space does not come easy and will often require that you sacrifice something in order to enjoy it. Learn to prioritize and enjoy these spaces and you'll find yourself ministering from the abundance of God's love and grace.

> *God, thank you for designing sacred tents and places of refuge in the craziness of life. I admit that I don't always feel like being with you, with others, or even with myself. But, your grace compels me to draw closer to you, and when I do, I am always blessed. So, teach me to embrace and enjoy every sacred space that you have ordained. Replenish my soul and prepare me for the great things you have in store. In Jesus' name. Amen.*

7

Mentorship

Mentorship in ministry is a crucial element of your success. With the right mentor, leaders like you can be guided, counseled, and discipled into becoming their best selves. There is rarely anyone, male or female, in a position of leadership who has not had a few mentors to mold him or her along the way. And, with the ever-changing landscape of ministry, women leaders not only need mentors but sponsors as well.

The difference between a mentor and a sponsor is simple: mentors help you to knock on the right doors, but sponsors help to open them for you. In fields where opportunities are often given to people who know the right people, mentors must also be sponsors who put their names behind those who are unknown so that others may know them. Those who are new to ministry can be sponsored into various networks simply because of a good mentor relationship.

I had always dreamed of having a mentor. I imagined that God would send me a woman in ministry who would take me under her wing and show me how to do everything that she did. I had witnessed this model with some of my male counterparts. There were pastors, professors, and even chaplains that took young men as students and mentored them into their fields. Pastors invited young men to hospitals, homes, and houses of faith, introducing them to others as sons. Professors invited male students to attend symposiums and guaranteed letters of recommendation for graduate school. I saw chaplains inviting men into apprenticeships where they could learn under the guidance of a seasoned chaplain. Aside from regular internships, these mentor relationships were really sponsorships.

For years, I would reach out to female pastors and ask if they would be my mentors and sponsors. I confess I was pretty bold and did not mind approaching women I respected to see if they had time for me. What I did not realize was that many of these women had so much on their plates that mentoring a new person was not something they could afford to do. They had to work hard to get where they were and, with exception of a few, most of the women I looked up to in ministry did not have the capacity to handle another relationship.

At first, I was discouraged. How could I get to the places to which I was called if no one would mentor me? Then it hit me. Maybe my understanding of mentorship was all wrong. Maybe I was looking for the wrong thing in the wrong place.

How to Choose the Wrong Mentor

If getting a mentor were easy, every leader would have one. But many women leaders do not. Some women in ministry simply do not have a whole lot of people to choose from as mentors. On top of that, the context of Christian leadership is often much more complex and political than other fields. Making a cold-call to a total stranger can leave you feeling more rejected than when you started. For this reason, many promising women will find themselves left out of the mentorship process and miss out on God's gift of learning from someone who's been there before. There may be hundreds of ways to get a good mentor, but there are also a handful of sure-fire ways to ensure that you don't.

How to Choose the Wrong Mentor:

1. Refuse to be mentored by someone outside of your network.

I knew what I was looking for. I wanted a woman pastor with a large network and time to teach me how to get where she

> Free yourself to embrace God-given mentors from a variety of places and in a broad array of fields.

was. Yet, while I was looking for something I did not have at that time, God was trying to show me what was already in my hand: My dad was a pastor and had already begun to recommend me for preaching engagements. My local pastor allowed me to tag along with him and even became my sponsor into international circles. My life coach was a minister and although she was not in my traditional network, she took me in and showed me all there was to know about coaching others. It was not until later in my career that God sent women who thought enough of me to be my mentors; even then, some did not look like me and one was in a different field altogether.

It's been said that people like people like themselves. This is also true for mentors. It is natural for us to think that women should have women mentors, racial minorities should have minority mentors, pastors should have pastors as mentors, and the like. Sometimes a diversified portfolio is healthy for your experience, not just your finances. You may need a minister as a mentor for pastoral care, but a businessperson can mentor you for church finances. You may look for a woman to mentor you through balancing family and work, but a male mentor could better help you navigate the politics of your denomination. You may want someone with a theological background as a mentor, but God may put someone with an administrative background in your life instead. Bottom line: don't limit yourself. Free yourself to embrace God-given mentors from a variety of places and in a broad array of fields.

2. Expect that your mentor will fix every problem that you face.

Karina had one of the best mentors you could ever ask for. She was always available to help her make tough decisions and opened doors for Karina's career that she could have never achieved on her own. Her mentor was like her angel—until Karina got fired. She was mad at everyone, but especially her mentor. Why didn't she help Karina keep her job? There must have been something that her mentor could have done to stop this from happening. When she confronted her trusted mentor, she heard this simple statement: sometimes you have to figure things out on your own. Karina was crushed and never contacted her mentor again.

Part of the reason why a good mentor is important is because they can help you avoid common mistakes. Yet, even when they give you the world's greatest advice, there are still other things that you must figure out on your own. Sure, the right mentor can see where you're headed and warn you about the pitfalls before you get there. But mentors are not God. They are human beings who (hopefully) provide godly wisdom at times when you need it. Every once in a while, God may use a mentor to help open doors or sponsor you into the right spaces at the right time. But even when that happens, mentors cannot speak into every area of your life at every time. If you want to keep a good mentor, manage your expectations and be prepared to measure every word of advice against your own meter of common sense.

3. Assume that your mentor exists to serve you.

Mentorship can easily become a selfish, one-way street. For mentors, the wrong mentee will require more from you than they give. The mentee will assume complete accessibility by contacting you more often than you can handle, assume exclusivity by demonstrating jealousy when you mentor others, and assume that you have no life outside of meeting their needs.

On the other hand, the wrong mentor will require more from his or her mentee than they are willing to give. They will make you work for a reward that always feels out of reach; make you give time or money for a cause that seems unrelated to your goals; or even force you to give up safe people or activities that threaten the mentor's authority over you.

To avoid having a selfish mentor or being a selfish mentee, set and keep clear boundaries at all times. Enter the relationship by agreeing on a set of clear expectations and honor the relationship by not crossing the lines. Honor your mentor's time by being honest about what you need. Take every opportunity to thank God for the people who care enough to invest themselves in your life. The right mentor will be thanking God for you as well.

4. Expect the mentorship relationship to last forever.

Dena felt so guilty when she decided to go to seminary. She was serving as the outreach ministry leader and had been mentored by her pastor's wife. For years, her pastor's wife had taken Dena under her wing, teaching her everything she needed to know about loving others and caring for herself. Dena never expected to leave that church, but when the door opened for her to go to seminary, she knew what she needed to do. She and her mentor agreed to maintain regular contact, but once classes started Dena found it nearly impossible with her class schedule to talk to her mentor each week. Slowly, their conversations became farther apart and before she knew it, several months had passed and they had not talked. Dena felt sad and ashamed that she had allowed the relationship to take a backseat. When she finally mustered the courage to call her mentor, she was relieved to hear that her mentor understood that she was in a new season of life. They agreed to end the formal mentorship and instead to try to connect whenever Dena was in town.

The wrong mentor will lead you to believe that he or she will be there forever. But, good mentors are given to us for a season. When you learn to see mentorship as an assignment, then you will know when it is completed. Bringing closure to a mentorship relationship may be hard, but it is a necessary part of growth. You'll never know if you can walk on your own if you always have crutches. Sometimes, God removes mentors through circumstances we did not anticipate. Other times, God will gently nudge you out of one mentor's care in order to further develop you with someone else. Regardless of the reason, it is wise to go into the mentor relationship expecting to learn and then moving on. When that time comes, celebrate the moment and allow closure to come naturally.

> You'll never know if you can walk on your own if you always have crutches.

Mentors are gifts from God. With the right guidance and sponsorship that mentors can provide, women can be catapulted into their callings with confidence and support.

Biblical Observations

> As I remember your tears, I long to see you, that I may be filled with joy. I am reminded of your sincere faith, a faith that dwelt first in your grandmother Lois and your mother Eunice and now, I am sure, dwells in you as well. For this reason I remind you to fan into flame the gift of God, which is in you through the laying on of my hands, for God gave us a spirit not of fear but of power and love and self-control. (2 Timothy 1:4–7 ESV)

Timothy was probably freaking out. He was one of the people being mentored by the apostle Paul, but the idea of pastoring a church on his own was undoubtedly scary. He had such a great relationship that his mentor considered him to be a son and ministry partner. Timothy had the privilege of traveling with Paul on some of his missionary journeys and was an eyewitness to the great things God did and said through him. Having studied Paul as his spiritual father, he was then invited to work alongside him in the spreading of the gospel. In fact, his name was mentioned in several of the letters that Paul wrote to others as a co-laborer and, in some cases, as coauthor.[1]

Timothy did so well under Paul's care that Paul recommended him to the church in Ephesus. He had served on the team long enough. It was now time for Timothy to pastor his first church. This kind of sponsorship was not something that Paul did on a regular basis. In order to ensure that the truth of the gospel would be preached, Paul was particular about who was selected. He knew that he could trust Timothy with the tasks of preaching the true gospel and extending Paul's legacy through Jesus Christ. It was the right thing to do, but it's clear that Timothy was uncertain. It's one thing to take on a task knowing that the more seasoned person is right there with you, but it's a whole new ball game to do it alone. After all that time together, Paul would not be there with Timothy for this new adventure. In fact, by the time he wrote the second letter to Timothy, Paul, the beloved mentor, was in prison. Yet, because of all that Paul had invested in his mentee, he was assured that the ministry of Christ would continue. Their relationship is proof that mentorship and sponsorship can be ordained by God to enhance our impact in the world.

Life Application

Ministry leadership can be scary. But, Paul shows us that *a good mentor can help you see what's already been invested in you.* Look at Paul's encouragement. He reminded Timothy of the faith that had been invested in him from his grandmother and his mother. He encouraged him to know that this very same faith was in him as well. If Timothy was unsure about his assignment, his mentor helped him to remember his faith legacy. Knowing that he was part of a rich lineage of strong faith was important in reassuring him that he was fit for the task.

Likewise, God has already invested so much in you: influence and power, faith and anointing for starters. *The right mentor will help you to recognize and fight against your fears.* Paul reminded Timothy that there was something more at stake. The most dominant enemy to Timothy's faith legacy was fear. Fear can cause you to abort your dreams and forfeit your calling. Instead, Paul reminds his mentee that God did not give him that fear. God gave him love, power, and self-control or soundness of mind.

While fear may be the first response, it does not have to have the last word. Fear may come at the onset of any new place in leadership, but it does not have to stay. When we operate in our God-given gifts and calling, we have the power to evict fear. Mentors who have been in similar places will remind us that we can get through fear with power, love, and sanity.

As you reflect on the role of a mentor for your life, consider the following questions:

1. Whom do you consider to be your mentor for this season of your life?

2. If you have a mentor, how can you maintain a productive relationship? If you do not have a mentor, what steps do you believe God wants you to take toward getting one?

3. What are the top three areas you want to work through with a mentor?

4. How can you pray for those who mentor you?

Summary

Everyone needs a mentor and women in leadership are no exception. Women in ministry need people who will mentor them through challenges and sponsor them into new opportunities. While it is easy to choose the wrong mentor, the right mentor relationship will serve as a blessing for us and for those connected to us. Mentors typically are with us for a season, until we outgrow a particular need.

Lord, thank you for the power that you have instilled in the mentorship relationship. I confess that I am in need of guidance and sponsorship as you lead me further in leadership. Please open my eyes to see the mentors you have already put in place and help me to respond to and care for them in a way that honors your name. Make me a mentor that holds nothing back, but gives generously to people of promise. In Jesus' name. Amen.

SECTION 3

LEAD WITH PURPOSE!

8

Finding your Place

You did it! You've embraced your calling and now you've come to the hard part: figuring out where to go next. For some women, this part is easy because they know where they are called to serve. Yet, for many other women, God's calling and preparing for it can be a little more ambiguous. They are not certain about the future and don't know if they should consider going to school, getting a license, becoming a candidate for ordination, getting a job, starting a nonprofit, forming a small group, teaching a Bible study, or a little of all of the above. This is why it can feel like it's the hard part. With so many options and so many ways to go, it can be hard to discern the trajectory of your call. This becomes even more challenging if you are in a context or denomination that does not ordain women or does not affirm the calling you have received. When you add the complexities of finances, location, politics, and family, it's easy to get to this point of discernment and simply want to turn around and walk away. In fact, there are lots of women who do.

Take Angela, for example. From a very young age, Angela knew that she had been called. She was a gifted speaker and was chosen for every lead part in her youth department since as far back as she could remember. Her pastor acknowledged her gifts as well and licensed her to preach within the context of the Baptist church. Excited and on fire for the Lord, she enrolled in seminary, knowing that he would be the first one to offer her a job when she graduated. When her final year came and went, she started to get a little nervous. She scheduled a meeting with her pastor and shared that she was ready to serve in full-time ministry but did not feel called to pastor a church. He encouraged her to look on various websites for opportunities and even suggested that she reach out to churches within the Baptist network for open positions. The bottom line for Angela was that she would not be getting the role she expected to have at her church. Discouraged and feeling disconnected, she still moved forward in putting out her résumé for

> God has designed specific places and spaces for every woman who says "yes" to the call.

jobs here and there. She had an occasional interview at a church, but was always turned down for lack of experience. With bills due and loans to pay, Angela decided to take a job in the mall until things panned out. She was the best-licensed preacher and M.Div. her department store had ever seen. With every passing month, Angela became more and more disheartened about serving in full-time ministry. She finally decided to give up her dream and settled for climbing the ladder in sales. She prayed that God would one day open the door for her fulfill her calling and put her degree and license to use.

While there are thousands of women who accept God's calling upon their lives to serve in some capacity of Christian leadership, there are many women who, like Angela, may never fully reach this goal. If we are not careful, we will see the obstacles to ministry service as closed doors without looking at how God may be opening windows on either side. But, I believe that God has designed specific places and spaces for every woman who says "yes" to the call. If this is the case, then there are no such things as a closed doors—only open doors (or windows) waiting to be found.

Candidacy, Licensure, Ordination, Oh My!

Since every denomination is different, the process to becoming recognized as a minister, preacher, elder, or pastor will be different as well. Some denominations require a training program that leads to a local church license to preach and teach. After receiving a license, these individuals are often candidates for ordination, depending on where they are called to serve. Other denominations consider a candidacy process for individuals who have passed various tests and are eligible for placement at churches within the denomination. Still other denominations only recognize women as evangelists, missionaries, or teachers, leading to another process altogether. While all of this may feel confusing, rest assured that the process to get where God is calling you to be can be very simple.

I remember the question my father asked me when I told him I felt God was calling me to ministry. He listened intently, affirmed my sense of call, and then it came out: "Have you talked to your pastor?" I was at a large church in Chicago at the time, hiding out in the back pew every Sunday and Wednesday night. As a preacher's kid, I was grateful for the gift of hiding in a church where no one really knew me, certainly not the pastor. "He doesn't even know me," I retorted, thinking that would be the end of the conversation. But with loving truth, my father helped me realize that I couldn't really take any next steps in my call without talking to the leaders in the church that had helped to cultivate and nurture that call, whether they knew me or not.

Generally, the first step in moving forward in your calling is to have a conversation with the pastor or appropriate church leader. This assumes, of course, that you have a regular place of worship and that you are under the care of a pastor, church, and denomination. If you are not currently in a place of worship, do what you can to find a place that fits who you are and what you feel called to do and be for the larger community. Join a congregation and become invested as a member. God's calling upon any life is never just for the individual. We respond to the call as a response to God meeting needs for the entire kingdom and communities of which we are a part.

This first step of speaking to your pastor or someone in leadership also assumes that you are in a place that affirms God's ability to use women in ministry. As progressive as many denominations claim to be, there are still many churches and denominations that do not believe women can be ordained to serve in areas of pastoral ministry or leadership. Some may agree on paper to women in ministry but hinder that calling in other ways, including lack of clarity around the timing or details of the process toward ordination. If you are called to serve the church and find yourself in this kind of setting, you must discern whether you are called to make an impact within the system or outside of it. Those who are called to make an impact within systems that do not recognize women in ministry should consider themselves as pioneers. They may gently push against the system from the inside, knowing that every crack in the glass brings us all one step closer to breaking the entire stained glass ceiling. They may deliver sermons from the floor, be asked to teach only women, or be commissioned as evangelists or missionaries without the title of minister or pastor. Those who are called to change systems from the outside may need to consider being ordained in an affirming congregation in order to fulfill God's calling for progress and change. Regardless of the limitations, women who are called to change closed systems from the inside and outside are necessary parts of God's plan.

Because every denomination is different, a conversation with the pastor or his or her designee can give you a perspective on what is required for candidacy, licensure, and ordination. Because not very Christian leader is called to preach, you may not need to seek licensure or ordination. You must decide for yourself whether you need to go this route by asking some questions:

1. What will it cost to pursue ordination in my current context?

2. Could I fulfill God's calling on my life without entering candidacy, receiving a license, and/or being ordained?

3. What more could God do through me if I went this route?

This decision is often most pertinent for women who sense God's calling to serve within the system of the church. Steps toward licensure and ordination are usually prerequisites to serving in pastoral leadership and, in some cases, chaplaincy as well. For example, if you feel called to make change within systems, churches, and institutions, you may do well to move forward with a path toward ordination. However, if you feel called to serve the community and to engage in work that is more missional (serving beyond the church) as opposed to congregational (serving within the church), you may not need to be ordained in order to accomplish your goals. Again, due to various denominational requirements and policies, a conversation with someone in leadership at your church will help to point you in the right direction.

To School or Not to School?

After accepting the call to ministry, I left my job in Chicago and moved to Charlotte, North Carolina. I knew that being a part of a training program where I could be licensed and prepared was critical to my own path of development. To be honest, I just wanted to get to the finish line as quickly as possible so that I could start teaching and serving in leadership. But, I kept feeling God calling me toward a journey of greater preparation and scholarship. It was around that same time that I knew my calling to ministry included going to seminary.

Seminaries are graduate schools that prepare men and women for Christian ministry. Divinity schools are usually graduate schools affiliated with universities. Depending on the school, their purpose can range from preparing individuals for Christian ministry to providing a broad-based study of religion. Bible colleges typically focus on undergraduate education with an emphasis on Christian ministry and practice. Bible Institutes, ministers' training programs, and the like are generally intended to provide enhanced knowledge of the Bible for people, regardless of previous education level. It is important to know the distinctions between schools so that you can choose the program that is right for you.

In some cases, a Master of Divinity degree is required for ordination. Other denominations may require training from the denomination or local church and see the degree as a plus. Increasingly, churches and religious institutions will honor and accept candidates with degrees that are not directly connected to religion. Education majors, finance experts, and MBAs are just as likely to be hired for certain roles as those with theological expertise. In other words, you don't necessarily have to do a theological degree in order to succeed in ministry. What preparation you need depends on the ministry and your denomination's requirements.

Many people see school as simply another step in the process of growing in one's relationship with Christ. They take undergraduate or graduate level classes in the same way that they would take an advanced Sunday school or Bible study course. But, a decision to pursue education (and spend significant money to do it) should not be considered lightly. It is a calling within itself and everyone called to ministry is not necessarily called to school. Likewise, everyone called to pursue this kind of advanced education may not be called directly to ministry leadership. For this reason, there are some key questions that must be answered before taking this step:

1. What level of education does my ideal position require?
2. What do I expect to gain from this educational experience that would better position me for my future?
3. If I did not go to graduate school, what would I miss?

For many women, the decision to attend seminary or divinity school is more than just about the educational experience. It is also an opportunity to expand one's network, broaden one's vocational horizons, and become exposed to the wider context of the Christian faith. Many of these institutions also provide opportunities to travel abroad, build ministry experience in a variety of contexts, lay a foundation for potential doctoral studies, and meet people who can serve as sponsors into other arenas after graduation.

Contrary to popular belief, you do not have to be a valedictorian to be successful in a graduate program. If you believe that God is calling you to pursue school, there are hundreds of programs and formats that can fit just about every learning style and stage of life. The key is discerning whether or not you are called in this direction, and if so, how God will open the doors to make this development part of your reality.

Getting a Job in Ministry

Before we begin this conversation about getting a ministerial job, we have to start by stating the obvious: not every job in ministry is paid. I know that makes some people cringe, but there are some who are called and are prepared to serve the church bi-vocationally—having a paid job in secular society and a volunteer leadership role at a church or community organization. Some women are called to teach public school and lead spiritual formation at a church. Some are called to work in administration and also pastor a church. This should not be overlooked as a viable calling and placement, especially considering factors such as church size, denominational limitations, and your own quality of life. If Paul was a tentmaker and still had time to minister and write edifying letters to his congregations, who's to say that you can't work your trade and do ministry at the same time?

When it comes to paid opportunities, ministry can feel like a closed, political playing field. In churches and denominations, it's all about whom you know and who knows you. For women fresh out of seminary or women discerning a call, getting a job can be challenging, but it is not impossible. Here are some ways to help your chances.

1. Pray. Sounds obvious, but it needs to be stated. God is the only One who will open the right doors for where you need to be. Without this critical step, you could mistake a good opportunity for God's opportunity and be filled with regret. Seeking God's guidance and direction before starting your job search takes off the weight of your finding something and puts it back on God's opening doors. In this way, you are simply trying the knobs to see where God is moving.

2. Serve where you are. The most common trend for hiring in churches is to hire from within. Most leaders already have someone in mind before the job description is even written or posted. Pastors and leaders prefer to hire (and promote) someone that already has the church's DNA, and those people are typically faithful in serving in volunteer positions or internships. By serving in a leadership position in your church, you will also build relevant experience and get recommendations from people who have seen your gifts in action.

> One of the most common mistakes that women make is waiting too late to build a network of influence.

3. Build your network early. One of the most common mistakes that women make is waiting too late to build a network of influence. Don't wait until your last year of seminary or the final leg of your training to start building relationships with people in leadership. Start as soon as you can. Schedule coffee, make phone calls, and plan in-person visits to find out more about how people got to where they are, what advice they can offer you, and what information they have about what's out there. Once the meeting is over, send a formal thank you and don't be afraid to attach your résumé in case the person with whom you met comes across an opportunity that is right for you.

4. Put yourself out there. Women are often the last ones to reach out to people they know and ask about opportunities to minister. We are usually not the ones to offer ourselves as speakers for church events, organizers for retreats, and candidates for open positions. However, if you don't speak up for yourself it might not happen that someone else will. Offer yourself as a speaker for women's day, apply for jobs online, volunteer to be a consultant for an organization, put together a proposal (with or without pay) to begin doing the ministry you feel called to do, and even hand-deliver a résumé packet with a CD of your most recent sermon to an open church. In short, take a leap of faith and go the extra mile to make yourself known. It may feel awkward at first, but those who take this leap are rarely disappointed.

5. Keep an open mind. Perhaps you have always envisaged yourself as a pastor, but if God opens a door for you to serve as a chaplain on a college campus, be willing to take it. Some positions are ideal for building skill sets that will help you later in your career. Just be careful not to get stuck in a position that you really don't want or for which you really aren't suited, thinking it will lead you to something else down the road. Be intentional about making your calling known and serve in such a way that your gifts are clear to everyone around you.

6. If the box doesn't fit you, build your own. There's a chance that doors may not open in established settings because God wants you to create your own. If you don't see a model or setting that fits you, you may need to create your own. This could be planting your own church, forming your own nonprofit, starting your own faith-based business, or anything else. There are plenty of successful women who started their own venture because existing structures did not fit what God called them to be and do. Understand that starting something on your own is not for the faint of heart. It should not be the option of last resort. Like anything else, it requires patience, diligence, faithfulness, and sometimes financing that only comes by the direction of the Holy Spirit. Those who are called to go in this direction can be assured that if God is with them, no obstacle will stop them.

Biblical Observations

Throughout Scripture, God is constantly reminding us of how our faithfulness in one area will make way for greater things to come. This is one of the main themes found in the book of Ruth. Her story started out with a sad realization: her husband had died. At that point, Ruth made a choice to stay with her mother-in-law, Naomi, instead of going back to live as a widow with her family of origin. Without a husband or children, it would seem that Ruth's decision to stay with her widowed mother-in-law was not very wise. At best, the two women would find a community where they could live off the benevolence of others. Worst case, they would starve together and die. Yet for some reason Ruth felt drawn to stay with Naomi and the two of them went to Bethlehem at the beginning of the harvest. Knowing that they needed to survive, Ruth asked Naomi to allow her to glean the leftovers from the fields of one of her wealthy relatives. Agreeing to the idea, Naomi sent her to the field owned by her relative, Boaz. Ruth had no idea what to expect, but she went anyway, picking up whatever the reapers had left behind. Every day, she would go to work in the fields and return with food for Naomi and herself.

One day, while working in the field, Boaz noticed Ruth. He immediately took interest in her and ordered his workers to leave extra gleanings for her. He spoke to her, encouraging her to stay and offering his protection and favor. In the process of this favor, Naomi instructed Ruth to let Boaz know of her deeper interest. After a short negotiation with Naomi's family, Boaz married Ruth and in time they became the great-grandparents of King David.

Life Application

You're probably thinking, "What does Ruth have to say about me getting a job?" The answer: a lot, actually. Through the story of Ruth, we learn key themes about God's favor in our faithfulness that will help us to discern next steps, even in employment.

If Ruth could speak to you right now, she'd probably tell you to *remain faithful where you are.* She had an opportunity to go on an unknown assignment, but she chose to stay where she was. This is sometimes a hard choice to make, but Ruth probably felt that she still had more care to offer her mother-in-law. Sometimes, we look outside to find open doors when the right ones have been in front of us the whole time. Be sure to exhaust your resources and finish the assignment where you are before you move to the next one.

Our sister Ruth may also tell us *not to despise small beginnings.* She started out as a poor gleaner, picking up the scraps of grain that the harvesters had overlooked. She didn't even have a real job or place among the servants. But it was while she was serving in this context that she was noticed and gained favor for a future that was more than she imagined. Ministry is filled with such small beginnings. No one who preaches to thousands started out that way. Very few people who dreamt of impacting whole communities actually began their journey that way. Most great women in ministry started with three people in a Bible study, two people in a room to pray, or even just themselves with a Bible and a plan to be faithful to God's calling. On your journey, remember that it's not how you start, but how well you live the journey for the glory of God.

Through her life story, Ruth teaches us that *getting a job is not about position, but about purpose and the fulfillment of God's plan.* By serving in her context, Ruth gained position among the reapers and even got the position of being wife to Boaz. But, at the end of the day, Ruth's life was not about her position, her title, her salary, or the size of her team. Ruth's life was about purpose and the role the she played in God's story. Through her, God fulfilled God's plan to bring joy to Naomi, extend the legacy through Boaz, and bring a king to the people of Israel.

That's an important point: you are not your job. Your life is not the sum total of the titles on your résumé. Your worth is not determined by the size of your church, the success of your organization, or even the number of people who joined the body of Christ through your leadership. Your life is all about God's purpose and the fulfillment of God's plan. With that in mind, you can be confident that God will secure a place for you to serve as a leader, not just for your benefit, but because there's a pretty good chance that God's plan depends on it. As you process these observations, think about the following questions:

1. If I put my fears aside, where and in what context do I believe God is calling me to serve?

2. What am I willing to risk in order to get the position to which I am called?

3. How can I be faithful where I am until I get where I am going?

4. What is God calling me to do right now?

Summary

Taking the first steps toward employment in ministry can feel daunting. If you're not in the inner circle, it can feel as if you'll never get to where you want to be. But if you are truly called, God will provide a place for you to maximize your gifts for God's glory. Get clarity on what's involved in licensure, ordination, and candidacy by talking to your pastor and leaders. Include others in your discernment process because it's easy to fool ourselves. Discern whether or not God is calling you to school. Take a few steps to build a firm foundation toward a successful career. Before you know it, God will make a clear path for your calling and set you in the right place to make eternal impact.

Lord, I believe you have a place that is just for me. I believe you have people waiting to receive the gifts and calling you have invested in my life. Holy Spirit, lead and guide me in the direction of your calling. Help me not to be discouraged by the obstacles that will come on the way to my purpose. When I get to the place you have for me for this season, surround me with peace in knowing that I've done the right thing and that I'm in the right place. I trust you, wholeheartedly. Amen.

9

Owning Your Body

I wish this chapter were not necessary and that issues about our bodies were shed like snakeskin when we accept God's call. I wish women in the church were assessed by the content of their character and not their bodies and their clothes. I have no greater desire for myself and for all of the women serving as leaders in ministry than to be free to be who we are without being critiqued by others. But, until the world ceases to see women as objects of beauty and desire, we will have to deal with the part of ourselves that is most often despised and desired: our bodies. Until the world changes how we view the physicality of the female body, those who are called to lead in ministry will have to wrestle with how we choose to show up in our bodies as we serve.

> It could be argued that a woman's body is the main reason why some men keep women from serving in leadership.

It could be argued that a woman's body is the main reason why some men keep women from serving in leadership. Our menstruating, potentially childbearing bodies lack the biological makeup of men and for that reason many people, men and women, have decided that it is not God's will for women to minister. But, let's be honest. The history of over-sexualization and over-objectification of women's bodies has also led many to believe that women are symbols of all that "real Christians" are taught to reject. The way we walk, the way we smell, the way we style our hair, the way we talk, and the clothes we wear have all been points of contention for men (and women) in the church who are trying to stay focused on God.

I've actually heard people say that a woman in the pulpit is a distraction because men and women are drawn to details about women (jewelry, hair, shoes, and so forth) that they would never notice about a man. This is sad, but it makes sense given that we are socialized to believe that women are to be seen, men to be heard. This myth plays out in leadership as both men and women tend to be more aware of a woman's looks and features. If men are to be heard, the way a man looks has very little to do with how he is received in leadership. For the most part, he will still gain respect whether he is tall or short, fat or skinny, attractive or unattractive. If women are to be seen, then how she looks can make a difference in how she is received as a leader. This is the rub. While it should not matter what we look like, we cannot ignore the world in which we live. Although we must find a space of being comfortable in our own skin, we must also wrestle with ensuring a seamless integration between who we are and how we present ourselves to the world.

Why This Matters

Gloria hated people noticing her. Growing up, she was considered the pretty one among her siblings and would get special favors from adults in the family. Everyone told her to consider modeling, and for a while she thought that was the best thing she could do. She competed in pageants and even won several titles before getting to high school. Yet, when she accepted the call of God on her life, everything changed. She shifted from focusing on her looks to focusing on her goals in ministry. When she entered the candidacy process for her denomination, she found herself struggling again with the way people looked at her. Once, after preaching at another church, someone came up to her and commented about how beautiful her hair looked as she delivered her sermon. On another occasion, someone told her they were so distracted by her smile that they didn't even hear the sermon. She even overheard a male pastor telling one of his deacons that he would never hire someone who looked better than his wife. These and other experiences left Gloria feeling uncomfortable and depressed. She couldn't help feeling as if her looks were a hindrance for the work she was called to do.

Dana never felt comfortable in her body. With weight fluctuations, bold features, and regular hair battles, she was constantly aware of all that was wrong. She ran from mirrors and avoided her reflection in the glass windows of the community center where she worked. She was good at what she did. She was called to serve the homeless population and although she hated what she looked like, she loved how she felt when she served people in need.

One morning at work, three of her coworkers surprised her with a gift card to a local hair salon. Dana was mortified. The fears and shame she carried about how she looked were all brought to light. Her coworkers' gesture confirmed her deepest fear: that other people saw what she saw. They all shared her disappointment with her body. Fighting back tears, she thanked them for the gesture, packed her bags, and went home. She began looking for another job that week.

June and her husband had tried for years to get pregnant and their prayers were finally answered. She was five months pregnant with a healthy baby girl! She was also serving as an associate pastor at a church. The joy of her pregnancy slowly faded when she was faced with comments she never expected from people she barely knew. Morning sickness in the pulpit forced her to share the news sooner than she wanted. Everyone celebrated and the pastor even made a comment that it was good to see the associate pastor fulfilling God's command to "be fruitful and multiply." She knew in that moment that her pregnancy would be evidence of her sexuality. From that point on, things became progressively worse. It was not uncommon for people to touch her belly, comment on how big or how small she looked, or suggest she not color her hair for fear that the chemicals would affect her unborn child. At the end of a leadership meeting one night, one of the men told her he loved seeing pregnant women and a woman within earshot violently dissented, sharing that pregnant women remind her of the child she lost. During the church cookout, someone offered to buy her a new bra for her ever-increasing chest and another person suggested she was wearing the wrong shoes to support her belly. What started out as a beautiful personal experience quickly turned into a painful and public one. As her pregnancy progressed, June grew increasingly uncomfortable with the weekly comments and talked with her husband about taking an early maternity leave. She could not stand the fact that her changing body had become public discourse.

All of us carry issues about our bodies into ministry and all of us will encounter others who will bring out the very things we want to hide. Yet, with God's grace it is possible to love your body and refuse to allow others' perceptions elicit shame.

Preacher Perspectives

The ramifications of a woman's body in ministry are endless. So much depends on your denomination, clergy attire requirements, size, height, and even the leadership role you play or to which you aspire. Since these variables change in almost every situation, perhaps the best thing to do is to understand various perspectives and locate ourselves within them. The following section attempts to do just that. It represents a variety of voices of women in ministry. While there is no single standard for how we carry our bodies within the church, the women's voices that follow represent the various ways that we can express who we are without shame.

Shoes

"I have to wear a robe every Sunday, but I love dressing up. Wearing designer black heels is my way of expressing myself within the confines of my tradition. "

"On most Sundays, I feel like I'm running a marathon. Seriously, when I wear my Fitbit, I get like eleven thousand steps in before 4 pm! Needless to say, I opt for comfortable shoes. Whether preaching or serving, a nice pair of black flats should be a staple for every woman in ministry."

Makeup

"I was never a makeup person before ministry and I'm still not much for it now. After starting at the church, I did decide to put on lip gloss every once in a while because I was tired of older people telling me my lips look naked when I speak."

"I don't leave the house without makeup. The key for me is making sure I have a black towel or handkerchief when I serve because I sweat like nobody's business! I learned this the hard way when I looked at my white towel and saw half my face on it. Never again!"

Hair

"Headbands are my thing, especially after someone told me they were distracted by how often I put my hair behind my ear. I was thinking, '*Yes, but did you hear anything I had to say?*'"

"I say as long as it looks nice, do what works best for you. The main thing for me is to make sure it's not in the way."

"I'm always conscious of my hair. One of the associates at my church is always doing something different, and when she does, I can count on at least four or five people in the congregation to do the same. If she colors, they color. If she cuts, they cut. It just makes me aware that whatever I do needs to be something I want others to imitate."

Nails

"During my honeymoon, I decided to get blue nails. I completely forgot I had them and went to preach for a youth conference. You should have seen the number of girls that came up to me asking about the color. I guess it was a big hit for the right crowd."

"My tradition says that your nails have to be neutral, so I pretty much stick with that. They say nothing, however, about your toenails. I think I have three different colors on today."

Clergy Attire

"I have to wear a clergy collar almost everyday. Since my wardrobe is already decided, I like to spice things up with colorful jackets, purses, and accessories."

"If I have my choice, I prefer to create my own preaching clothes. Because of my size, I've found that a loose blouse and a fitted skirt are better for my figure than a straight cassock or robe."

"In my tradition, a woman must have a cloth to cover her lap if her skirt comes above the knee when she sits down. This is the case with just about everything I own, so I finally broke down and bought a few long skirts. Not only do they look nice, but they keep me from carrying another thing around."

Women in ministry represent a broad spectrum of style and grace. Whether fashion-forward or comfort-bound, we make up a beautiful tapestry of how ministry looks and feels. As we embrace who we are bodily, we give others strength to do the same.

Biblical Observations

God put on flesh. This is the truth that baffled the trained religious leaders and surprised those who were convinced that goodness only existed in the spirit. Jesus Christ, the Son of God, came to earth enrobed in flesh. He could have chosen any number of forms to embrace for this earthly encounter.

But, Jesus made flesh his garment of choice. Existing in divine relationship with God as the Word who was with God and in God and was God, Jesus decided that the best and only way to engage with creation was in flesh.

> Jesus became flesh, birthed from Mary's flesh, to dwell with and save flesh-covered people.

The significance of this Incarnation, no matter how mysterious, can never be overlooked. John clearly states, "The Word became flesh and dwelt among us" (John 1:14 NKJV). He came with hangnails and toe jam, earwax and morning eye crust. Jesus came in flesh; flesh that was capable of cellulite, love handles, moles, freckles, scars, and drastic imperfections. He chose to come in the same bodies that cause so many hang-ups and to be with people who would be forever flawed with bodily shame from the Garden of Eden. But, he still came, in flesh, to be with flesh.

Not only did Jesus come in flesh, he also came through flesh, through human birth. Jesus became flesh, birthed from Mary's flesh, to dwell with and save flesh-covered people.

Life Application

The fact that Jesus came in flesh affirms so much for women. First, *Jesus' birth affirms women's bodies as vessels of God's Word.* That he was born through Mary validates women's bodies as capable of carrying and birthing God's Word, which is Christ. In this process, God acknowledges and perhaps even validates our cycles and our hormones and our seasons and our changes. All that makes us female is validated through the birth of Christ. After all, what more is a preacher than one who carries and birth's God's Word?

This mysterious act of *Jesus taking on flesh also affirms that we are called to the ministry of representing God in flesh.* In ministry, we often try to hide behind the cross, supposedly so that others may see God and not see us at all. As women, we may secretly wish away our features in order for people to "see more of God." Yet this scripture suggests that in doing so, we miss the whole point of Jesus becoming flesh. For someone, somewhere, the "more" that God wants to show them will come through you. Being made in God's image as a woman, you are an ambassador and representative of a God who chooses to be revealed through flesh of men and of women. When you deny your body, which was fashioned in God's image, you are denying God.

In this meaningful passage, *Jesus also affirms the idea that our bodies are symbols of God's redemption.* Thank God for that! The purpose of Jesus coming in flesh was to redeem flesh. Jesus did not die so that we could have perfect bodies on earth. Instead, the death of Christ on the cross redeems our bodies from the shame of sin and refashions us for God's glory, both now and for the time to come.

So, although you may not like what you see in your body, you've still been bought with a price.[1] Because of Jesus, our bodies are now temples of the Holy Spirit and will one day be redeemed when we are gathered together with him.[2] If this is the case, my beloved sister, you are no longer allowed to have body-bashing sessions about yourself or anyone else. If you have truly been purchased by God, then your body is no longer yours alone, which gives you no right to put yourself down. We now have a responsibility to learn to love God with our bodies by being good stewards over what we've been given. As women of God, our charge is to lead in moving from shame to grace in our God-given flesh.

As you consider the importance of your body, think about the following questions:

1. What stands in the way of your accepting your body as you are?
2. What do you love most about your body?
3. What does it look like for you to show love for God by taking care of your body?

4. How is God calling you to affirm others to move from shame to grace in their bodies?

Summary

While it is easy to despise our bodies, God encourages us to embrace them. As women in ministry, our challenge is to find the best ways to show up in our flesh in all that we do. Our unique styles can shine through any personality and encourage others to do the same. Scripture reminds us that Jesus affirms us as vessels of the Word, representatives of God, and symbols of Christ's redemption. The best thing we can do for ourselves and for the body of Christ is to own who we are and give God glory in our flesh.

God, I confess that I have not always been happy about my body. There are times when I reject the very things you affirm about me. Help me to love the body you've given me. Give me strength and grace to take care of this temple like it's yours. Most importantly, let the witness of my journey be encouragement for some young girl to love her body without shame. Amen.

10

Passion in Your Back Pocket

Once upon a time, there was an anointed young woman who was called to serve the church in full-time ministry. After graduating from school, this anointed young woman got a job serving as a pastor at a wonderful church. She was paid relatively well and had enough to live a comfortable lifestyle. She gave her all to the church, being sure to keep outside engagements and opportunities to a minimum.

In addition to being a gifted preacher, teacher, and pastor, she was also a gifted cook. It was not uncommon for her to host gatherings at the church and prepare all of the food. On several occasions, she was invited to turn her culinary skills into additional revenue. But, for fear of neglecting her primary duties as pastor, she poured all of her gifts into that one place. She preached, prayed and cooked in that one congregation. The people loved her and took in everything that she poured out.

Years went by and this anointed young woman became an anointed older woman. When it was time for her to retire, she was informed that neither the church nor the denomination had anything set aside for her to live on. What they had been saving for her retirement gift they had spent on building repairs a few years back. With nothing else to lean on, this anointed older woman began to think about all of the gifts she had poured into that place. Saddened and desperate, she remained where she was and took her last breaths serving in the church.

> Our lives are so dynamic that no one place is designed to hold it all.

This unfortunate tale is the reality for many men and women in ministry. Adhering to the thinking that all of our gifts were intended for one place often keeps us from exploring the many passions we have been given. The fullness of life is best experienced in a variety of contexts. This is especially true for women in ministry leadership. Because of the unpredictable nature of ministry, wise women will always have other passions and skill sets to lean on that will enhance what they bring to the church. This is not to say that following God requires a plan B. It is a simple understanding that every gift that God gives is not *just* for the church. Some gifts that God gives to those who serve in ministry are designed to complement or even offset ministry in a manner that enhances the kingdom and gives glory to God.

Here's another honest truth: ministry can sometimes feel restrictive, especially when you're not getting paid much to do it. When your life is filled with meeting the needs of others, you can feel as if your worth is restricted to the success of your last event, the applause from your last sermon, and the satisfaction of those you serve. In addition, not every woman in ministry will have the opportunity to serve in a full-time capacity. But, having passions and desires outside of ministry reminds you that you are not only defined by your ministry. You are more than just the person who meets everyone's needs. You are a whole person who was designed to impact the world in a variety of significant ways. Our lives are so dynamic that no one place is designed to hold it all. You were not designed only to walk. You were also created to fly! Cultivating your gifts and talents outside of the local context allows you to spread your wings and fly above what's in front of you to explore a bigger life beyond. It allows you to see yourself beyond what you do and recognize your worth based on the fullness of who you are—and maybe even make some extra money doing it!

The Financial Outlook of Ministry

"Never put yourself in a position where income from the church is all you have." This was the advice my dad gave me when I got my first job in ministry. I was so happy finally to get paid for what I had been doing as a volunteer. When I shared the news with him, I expected he would be excited about what I was making. Instead, he pushed me on to keep thinking and not settle for what I had. When I preached at other churches and received an honorarium, he advised me to put that money into my savings and not consider it part of my regular budget. After several years of testing my own theories, I realized he was right.

The reality is that many churches, nonprofits, and religious institutions will struggle with their finances. While God will always provide for the church, the future of paying healthy salaries for those who serve God's church is unclear. There was a time when those who went into ministry would not only get a salary but also housing allowance, car allowance, continuing education stipend, benefits, and a guaranteed cost of living increase. More recently, however, many churches have cut back on these allowances. In some cases, it's because they cannot afford them and in other cases, it's because they no longer see them as necessary. Some churches have put everything together and called it a "salary package," making those who accept such positions feel as if they are getting much more than they really are. Because finances are such a sensitive topic for institutions that survive based on the goodwill of others, some ministers find that they have no one to talk to when it comes to fair pay.

In addition, many women in ministry have discovered that where you start in your salary is typically where you stay.

Barring promotions to other positions or explosive growth of the congregation, churches and religious institutions rarely give increases. If you're not intentional, you could start out very comfortable and end up ten years later financially stressed. These issues are compounded when you add school loans, family needs, credit cards, mortgage, rent, and a steady increase in the cost of living.

Adding further to the financial picture is the fact that women still make less on the dollar than men. Unfortunately, the situation is no different in the church. There are hundreds of examples of women in ministry who have the same or more responsibility than others and yet make less than their counterparts. Single women may find that not having a family factors into the salary decisions for some boards, keeping them at lower salaries than that of a man with a wife and children. This injustice is enough to make some women leave the church altogether. But, as with all things that require faith, there is a reason to have hope. While there are some situations in which it is best that you pack up and leave, there are other times when God will give you the tools you need to grow from where you are.

From Passion to Profit

Christine was known for her artistic gifts. In fact, she was a full-time art teacher when she first entered the ministers training program at her church. She also led the visual arts ministry as a volunteer, and when the opportunity came for a staff position, she was eager to apply. Christine went through three rounds of the interview process and was thrilled when the church offered her the position. There was only one problem: the salary at the church was much less than what she was making as a teacher. There was no way she could keep her current job and take on the church position as well. Deep down, she knew that God was calling her to take on this new church role, so she took the leap of faith and began working at the church.

A few months into her role, she remembered the blog she had started for Christian artists. It was something she had done on the side but had never taken the time to develop. She decided to put some time into developing the blog after work and on weekends. Before long, the blog grew and a community of about two thousand people subscribed each week to see her work and hear what she had to say. Although she never considered this space as anything other than personal expressions and thoughts, her subscribers saw things differently. As she posted her artwork, people inquired about purchasing it and a bidding war began. Soon, Christine's passion turned into revenue that she used to complement her salary. By the end of that year, she was making more from her job at the church and her blog than she had as a full-time art teacher.

Christine's story represents so many women in ministry who have found ways to turn their passion into profit. Whether our passions comprise our full-time jobs, our part-time jobs, or our side hobbies, we can use them for God's glory and the benefit of the wider community. So what makes a profitable passion?

1. **Profitable passions are usually solutions to others' problems**. They usually meet a need or fill a void that others have. Think of how your gifts answer questions others are asking.

2. **Profitable passions are in line with who you are and the impact God has called you to make**. Whatever you decide to do on the side should enhance and not take away from who you are in ministry. While your passions can be expressed in a variety of ways, they should not take away from your witness for Christ.

3. **Profitable passions are sustainable over time and transferable between spaces**. This should not be a "one hit wonder," but something that you can do that goes with you wherever you are. Your passion should not be contingent on a specific time or place.

4. **Profitable passions are things that come easily and flow naturally out of your gifts**. Think of things that you do naturally. You may find that God has given you an additional source of revenue from something that you're already doing or something that you absolutely love to do.

5. **Profitable passions may require an initial investment, but potentially bring exponential returns**. Some passions may involve a cost for training that will come back to you once your passion gets going. Such is the case with becoming trained with a specific skill, educated in a certain field, or certified with a specialized license.

Turning your passion into profit will take time and effort. Not everyone has the energy to focus on more than one thing at one time. However, those who decide to explore their passions beyond the pulpit will enjoy the gift of experiencing God in more than one context. They will have the ability to be free from the confines of a nonprofit salary and may be able to give more than they previously could.

In addition to bringing in profit, your passions can help to keep you grounded and well rounded in leadership. Profitable passions will prove that you can preach and write books, build communities and be a banker, pray and teach dance, lead and be a life coach, minister and produce music. No matter what you choose, you should know that you have been given skills that extend beyond what you do in ministry to the church. It's up to you to determine what you do with those skills and how you make them work for you.

Biblical Observations

> And on the Sabbath day we went out of the city to the riverside, where prayer was customarily made; and we sat down and spoke to the women who met there. Now

a certain woman named Lydia heard us. She was a seller of purple from the city of Thyatira, who worshiped God. The Lord opened her heart to heed the things spoken by Paul. And when she and her household were baptized, she begged us, saying, "If you have judged me to be faithful to the Lord, come to my house and stay." So she persuaded us. . . . So they went out of the prison and entered the house of Lydia; and when they had seen the brethren, they encouraged them and departed. (Acts 16:13–15, 40, NKJV)

Lydia was a well-known businesswoman. She sold dyed fabrics in the city and it is likely that most people knew who she was. She was successful at what she did and made a good name for herself. But her legacy really began when she encountered the gospel of Jesus Christ. Hearing the message from Paul, this businesswoman was compelled to turn her allegiance to the Lord. Most theologians agree that she became the first recorded convert in Europe. Her open heart prompted open doors when she invited Paul and his followers to stay with her.

Sure, Lydia was a businesswoman, but she became a believer as well. Her faith in God became her most dominant feature as she grew in her relationship with God. The one who once led in the marketplace would soon lead in the religious arena, turning her house into a meeting place for God's people. She started out gathering with the women at the riverside, but by the end of the chapter she was the one who gathered men and women in her home. Some have said that this businesswoman turned into a pastor and formed a worshipping community in her house. Since these house churches brought in very little money, we can speculate that she kept her marketplace business as well. If so, there would be no doubt that her passion as a businesswoman added to her faith leadership. She would need financial acumen to know how to distribute gifts for missionaries and the poor. She would use her marketing sense to spread the news about what God was doing. Her business skills impacted her ministry, but her ministry impacted her business as well. Certainly, her pastoral care would play into deals being made, items being exchanged, and merchandise being purchased. At the end of the day, it was all for God's glory. Whether selling fabric or sharing the good news, Lydia operated out of her passion for God that paid off in numerous ways for all.

Life Application

Lydia is a beautiful example of a woman in ministry leadership who kept her profitable passion. Through her, we are reminded that *we do not have to forsake our gifts to embrace our call.* God can use all of our gifts and skill sets to enhance and complement the ministries we've been given. Lydia's impact was so great because she used her skills to develop something wider than herself. By the time she was converted, she had a house, a secure business, and influence that very few women had. God was able to use all that she had to make the gospel attractive to many. The same will be true of some women who accept God's calling while working secular jobs. You may think that what you do is no longer important, but the opposite is true. If God allowed you to have a job prior to accepting the call to ministry, then God must have plans to build upon and expand your influence there. Lydia reminds us that you don't have to quit your day job to follow God with your whole heart. God can use all that you have built to bless you and benefit others.

> Lydia reminds us that you don't have to quit your day job to follow God with your whole heart.

Lydia's story also reminds us that *our gifts make room for the gospel.* Did you notice how she started out with women, but ended with a mixed group of men and women? Because she was skilled in business, she was able to have a home that could be used as a meeting place for believers. Her passion for God and news of her conversion made room for her to do so much more than sell fabric. She may never have imagined that her business would be an open door for God or that God would make full use of her business, but it happened for her and will happen for you. God can use your gifts to make more room for the gospel. God can expand your clothing line to extend your witness. God can formalize your fitness training as a platform for truth. God can grow your makeup business, allowing you to minister to the deeper needs of more of your clients. Whatever your gift, God can use that passion as a launching pad into the truth of the gospel.

As you consider Lydia's story, think about the following questions for your own life:

1. Where do you want to be financially in five and ten years?
2. What will it take to get there?
3. What passions and gifts has God given you that can be developed into additional profit?
4. What difference will your profitable passions make for you and/or other people?

Summary

The financial future of nonprofit institutions is not certain. No matter where we are in ministry, we cannot afford to be comfortable with one stream of income. Wise leaders will invest time and effort into developing a passion that can be turned into profit, for the glory of God. Take the time to assess what you have been given and make the most of every gift and opportunity. This discipline will not only benefit you as a well-rounded leader, but also can generate revenue to bless you and those to whom you are called to minister.

Lord, I thank you for all of the gifts, talents, and skills you have invested in my life. Thank you for calling me not only to serve the church but also to live my life for you beyond this one context. Grant me wisdom to maximize the gifts I've been given for your glory. Show me places where you desire that I turn my passions into profit and expand my vision to see the impact you want to make through me. I give myself to you, totally and completely. Make me a good steward over this life. In Jesus' name. Amen.

Epilogue

Alise always knew that she would be a pastor. As a child, she would use toilet paper rolls for microphones and bath towels for church robes. Her congregations varied from dolls to stuffed animals to family members and friends who would patiently listen to her "preach" about Jesus. Throughout school, she found herself talking about God in almost every context and her convictions were strong. She was constantly affirmed by her community and was elected to serve as the youth assistant to the pastor by the age of twelve.

With support from her pastor, family, and leaders, Alise graduated from seminary and became a pastor at a midsized church. She led with passion and authority and it was clear to everyone that she was made for this unique calling. Although her work was not without challenges, she handled them with grace. When faced with tough decisions, Alise grounded herself in God. In the midst of congregational disputes, she modeled the effectiveness of prayer and reconciliation. She was successful by anyone's standards and carried more accomplishments than her office wall could hold. But, if you asked her what made her most proud, she would tell you two things: First, she was proud that God allowed her to do what she always felt called to do. Second, she was honored to teach young girls that they were made for positions of leadership in the church and also in the world.

Alise represents what can happen when young women truly believe that they were made for leadership in the church. Her story represents the tip of an iceberg made up of strong women and confident men who aren't afraid to walk confidently in their callings. These leaders will stand on the shoulders of women who had to take the floor instead of the pulpit, but preached the gospel without shame. They will rest on a foundation made up of women who fought for justice, absorbing bruises on the outside, but refusing to allow their souls to be wounded. Alise represents the stories of women raised by mothers who never questioned if they belonged, but sat at the table knowing that God designed them with something meaningful to offer. She signifies what can happen when we women stop asking for permission and start leading with the gifts that God has given us.

This can be our future and the future can be now. The moment a woman begins to walk in the fullness of God's calling for her life is the moment that God initiates a ripple effect of blessings that flow from her to her inner circle, to her community, and into the world. By taking one small step of faith, God creates impact that expands exponentially beyond what can happen through any one life. If this is indeed the case, then the question we ask ourselves cannot be, Should I go where God is leading? The question any woman leader must ask should be, What will happen if I *don't* go where God is leading?

If you don't go, some family may never experience what equality looks like in the body of Christ. If you don't go, some community will be robbed of the unique gifts that God has invested in you. If you don't go, you will forever feel stifled and trapped by a world of regret, remorse, and dispassionate living. By not going where God is leading, you may silence the voice of the Holy Spirit within you and dampen the fire that God has set in your bones. Young women may never see a woman in the pulpit. Young men may never see women as capable of fulfilling the call of leadership. The world will see secular careers advancing in opportunities for women while the church remains stagnant. Congregations may never be pushed outside of the box of masculine leadership and paternalistic interpretation. My sister, if you don't go, God will send someone else, but all of us will miss out on what God could have done through you.

When I was in school, we used to play the Dare Game. We

would dare each other to do things that seemed crazy in order to win the unspoken title of the most daring girl in the class. Unfortunately, I was crazy enough to take dares and even double dares because I wanted to be popular and stand out. What I didn't know at the time was that God had already issued a dare that would change my life. It was the dare to take on the call of leadership that I did not think was possible for me. God issued a challenge for me to assume authority and responsibility in the church with the same determination that I had in the world. I'm proud to tell you that I took that dare and I'm still taking the dare daily, striving to live out God's purpose for my life and leadership in God's church.

I don't know what your dare looks like, but if you are called to lead, God is daring you to take risks. You are called to do what others think is impossible and to go where some would say is unthinkable. It may not always feel comfortable, but if you accept the dare, you will help to change the world.

My prayer for every reader is that you will heed the voice of the Lord speaking to your soul. I pray that you will not forsake the calling upon your lives to lead like you've never seen and go where you've never gone before. May God give you courage to embrace what has yet to be grasped, envision what has yet to be seen, and embark on a journey that has yet to be traveled: a journey that will lead you in the direction of God's will for your life and for the church as a whole.

You have what it takes to fulfill this calling. You are equipped with the mind-set to take on this task. You've been born with a penchant for the desires of God's heart. You can do this because you were, without a doubt, made for this.

Bibliography

Allen, Bob. "Report: Women Ministers Gaining Ground in Baptist Life," *Associated Baptist Press,* June 23, 2011. http://www.abpnews.com/archives/item/6509-report-women-ministers-gaining-ground-in-baptist-life.

Burton, M. Garlinda. "Women Pastors Growing in Numbers," *United Methodist News,* May 20, 2014. http://www.umc.org/news-and-media/women-pastors-growing-in-numbers.

Durso, Pamela R., and Amy Shorner-Johnson. *The State of Women in Baptist Life, 2010.* Baptist Women in Ministry, 2011. http://www.bwim.info/files/State_of_Women_in_Baptist_Life_2010.pdf.

Grenz, Stanley J. *Women in the Church: a Biblical Theology of Women in Ministry.* With Denise Muir Kjesbo. Downers Grove, IL: IVP Academic, 1995.

Lyons, Courtney. "Breaking Through the Extra-Thick Stained-Glass Ceiling: African-American Baptist Women in Ministry." *Review & Expositor* 110, no. 1, (December 2013): 77–91.

Religion Link Editor. "Women Clergy: A Growing and Diverse Community," May 15, 2015, http://www.religionlink.com/source-guides/women-clergy-a-growing-and-diverse-community.

Religious News Service. "Black Women Trying to Reach Pulpits Face Resistance: Clergy: Number of Seminary Students Is on the Rise, but Some Find the Ministry in African-American Culture Remains a Bastion for Men." *Los Angeles Times,* November 7, 1992. http://

articles.latimes.com/1992-11-07/local/me-1309_1_
black-women.

Sandberg, Sheryl. *Lean In: Women, Work, and the Will to Lead.*
New York: Knopf, 2013.

Notes

Introduction

[1]Isaiah 61:1a NRSV.

[2]Stanley J. Grenz, *Women in the Church: A Biblical Theology of Women in Ministry* (Downers Grove, IL: IVP Academic, 1995).

[3]Sheryl Sandberg, *Lean In: Women, Work, and the Will to Lead* (New York: Knopf, 2013), 66.

[4]This age group is also referred to as the "Millennial Generation."

[5]Sandberg, *Lean In,* 16.

[6]Joel 2:28-29, 1 Corinthians 12:4-11, Galatians 3:28.

[7]Pamela R. Durso and Amy Shorner-Johnson, "The State of Women in Baptist Life, 2010," Baptist Women in Ministry, June 2011, http://www.bwim.info/files/State%20of%20Women%20in%20Baptist%20Life%202010.pdf.

[8]Bob Allen, "Report: Women Ministers Gaining Ground in Baptist Life," Associated Baptist Press, June 23, 2011, http://www.abpnews.com/archives/item/6509-report-women-ministers-gaining-ground-in-baptist-life.

[9]M. Garlinda Burton, "Women Pastors Growing in Numbers," United Methodist News, March 20, 2014, http://www.umc.org/news-and-media/women-pastors-growing-in-numbers.

[10]Ibid.

[11]The term *deaconess* is a gender-specific term and refers to a job that often carries less responsibility than that of deacons or can refer to the unique responsibilities of women serving as elders in predominantly Baptist traditions.

[12]Religious News Service, "Black Women Trying to Reach Pulpits Face Resistance: Clergy: Number of Seminary Students Is on the Rise, but some Find the Ministry in African-American Culture Remains a Bastion for Men" *Los Angeles Times,* November 7, 1992, , http://articles.latimes.com/1992-11-07/local/me-1309_1_black-women.

[13]Courtney Lyons, "Breaking Through the Extra-Thick Stained-Glass Ceiling: African-American Baptist Women in Ministry" *Review & Expositor* 110, no. 1 (December 1, 2013): 77–91.

[14]Religion Link Editor, "Women Clergy: A Growing and Diverse Community," May 15, 2015, http://www.religionlink.com/source-guides/women-clergy-a-growing-and-diverse-community.

[15]Acts 2:17–18 NIV.

Chapter 1: Made for the Call

[1]1 Corinthians 14:34–35; 1 Timothy 2:9–15.

[2]A pseudonym.

[3]Genesis 16.

Chapter 6: Sacred Space

[1]1 Kings 18:20–40.

Chapter 7: Mentorship

[1]Romans, 1 and 2 Corinthians, Philippians, Colossians, 1 and 2 Thessalonians, and Philemon.

Chapter 9: Owning Your Body

[1]1 Corinthians 6:20.

[2]1 Corinthians 6:19, 1 Corinthians 15:51–53.

Printed and bound by PG in the USA

USA2010PG1L